T4-ABL-018

Breaking In

Breaking In

nine first-person accounts about becoming an athlete

compiled and edited by Lawrence T. Lorimer

illustrated with photographs

RANDOM HOUSE NEW YORK

Copyright © 1974 by Random House, Inc. All rights reserved under International and Pan-American Copyright Conventions. Published in the United States by Random House, Inc., New York, and simultaneously in Canada by Random House of Canada Limited, Toronto.

Library of Congress Cataloging in Publication Data
Lorimer, Lawrence T comp. Breaking in: nine first-person accounts about becoming an athlete. 1. Athletes—United States—Biography—Juvenile literature. I. Title. GV697.A1L67 1974 796′.092′2 [B] 73-18743 ISBN 0-394-82653-1 ISBN 0-394-92653-6 (lib. bdg.)

Designed by Grace Clarke

Manufactured in the United States of America 1 2 3 4 5 6 7 8 9 0

ACKNOWLEDGMENTS

I'M GOING TO BE A BALLPLAYER. Condensed from *The Glory of Their Times* by Lawrence S. Ritter. Copyright © 1966 by Lawrence S. Ritter. Reprinted by permission of Macmillan Publishing Co., Inc.

IT WAS MY WAY OUT. Adapted from *Stand Up for Something: The Spencer Haywood Story* by Bill Libby and Spencer Haywood. Copyright © 1972 by Bill Libby and Spencer Haywood. Reprinted by permission of Grosset & Dunlap, Inc.

COME AND TAKE ME HOME. From *The Education of a Baseball Player* by Mickey Mantle. Copyright © 1967 by Mickey Mantle. Reprinted by permission of Simon & Schuster, Inc.

WHY DIDN'T YOU THROW THAT RIGHT? From *The Original Sin: A Self-Portrait* by Anthony Quinn. Copyright © 1972 by Anthony Quinn. Reprinted by permission of Little, Brown and Co.

I WAS PLAYING FOR SURVIVAL. From *Out of Their League* by Dave Meggyesy. Copyright © 1970 by Dave Meggyesy. Reprinted by permission of Ramparts Press.

WHO OWNS A CHAMPION? and the quotation on pages 3–4. From *Deep Water* by Don Schollander and Michael Savage. Copyright © 1971 by Donald A. Schollander and Michael D. Savage. Reprinted by permission of Crown Publishers, Inc.

AN AMAZINGLY GENEROUS THING. Abridged and adapted from pages 26–57 of *I Always Wanted to be Somebody* by Althea Gibson. Copyright © 1958 by Althea Gibson and Edward E. Fitzgerald. Reprinted by permission of Harper & Row, Publishers, Inc.

I CAN USE MY LEFT! From *High Stick* by Ted Green with Al Hirshberg. Copyright © 1971 by Al Hirshberg and Ted Green. Reprinted by permission of Dodd, Mead & Company, Inc.

THE GUTS NOT TO FIGHT BACK. Condensed from *Wait Till Next Year: The Life Story of Jackie Robinson* by Carl T. Rowan with Jackie Robinson. Copyright © 1960 by Carl T. Rowan and Jack R. Robinson. Reprinted by permission of Random House, Inc.

PHOTO CREDITS

The Bettmann Archive, 19; Culver Pictures, 2, 69, 79; Robert B. Shaver, 167; Solon High School, 99; United Press International, 43, 59, 108, 123, 132; University of Detroit, 25; Wide World, 47, 84, 154, 158, 174, 195.

This book was made for my son Paul

CONTENTS

INTRODUCTION ■ xi

I'M GOING TO BE A BALLPLAYER
    Rube Marquard ■ 3

IT WAS MY WAY OUT
    Spencer Haywood ■ 23

COME AND TAKE ME HOME
    Mickey Mantle ■ 45

WHY DIDN'T YOU THROW THAT RIGHT?
    Anthony Quinn ■ 67

I WAS PLAYING FOR SURVIVAL
    Dave Meggyesy ■ 85

WHO OWNS A CHAMPION?
    Don Schollander ■ 107

AN AMAZINGLY GENEROUS THING
    Althea Gibson ■ 133

I CAN USE MY LEFT!
    Ted Green ■ 157

THE GUTS NOT TO FIGHT BACK
    Jackie Robinson ■ 173

INTRODUCTION

■When a promising young athlete enters major competition, he must learn to cope with many kinds of attention and pressure. Coaches, fans, and local newspapers hail him as a miracle-worker from the moment he wins his first game or race. The cheers grow louder as he proceeds through each level of his sport, from high school to the professional or Olympic team. As the praise grows, however, so does the pressure to keep winning.

As he moves up, the athlete is constantly facing unfamiliar situations and learning to cope with his excitement and apprehension. Will he succeed? What will happen if he fails? He must break in on new teams and meet increasingly stiff competition. He must learn from coaches and older competitors, and wait for a chance to get into the game and show his talent. If he succeeds, his reward is often another move up, and he must once again establish new routines, make new friends, and adjust to new surroundings. Finally, if the athlete does reach the top in his sport, he must learn to live as a celebrity and to survive gracefully under the steady pressure to prove himself again and again.

Breaking into any competitive profession is difficult. Actors and musicians soon learn the cost of winning and keeping a place in a performing group. Doctors, lawyers, policemen, and many others face more subtle kinds of competition and pressure during their training and early days on the job. But nowhere are the pressures so clear-cut as in big-time sports.

In this book nine athletes—eight men and one woman—tell what it was like to get started in the ruthlessly competitive sports world. In excerpts from autobiographical writings, they show the personal side of working to become a professional or world-class amateur athlete. They describe not only what they did but how they felt at the time—and how they felt years later looking back at their young selves. They are a remarkable group in many respects, and their stories illustrate the personal qualities necessary to become a successful athlete.

To begin with, an ambitious athlete must have enormous talent. And he must start young, in most cases committing himself to a sport by the time he is 16. Success depends heavily on speed, strength, and reflexes, so he must hurry to make good before his muscles and timing lose their youthful perfection. Swimmers often swim their fastest times before they are 20 and most other athletes reach their peaks before 30. The serious athlete must also grow up in a hurry, leaving home at an early age, entering major competition, and perhaps even becoming a celebrity in his teens or early twenties.

The next requirement is single-mindedness—an ability to set a goal and pursue it to the exclusion of everything else. Even the most talented competitor must spend thousands of hours conditioning himself and practicing his sport, sacrificing time that might otherwise be spent studying or just having fun. Coaches are fond of praising an athlete by saying, "He's willing to pay the price." The price of winning is living a life devoted to the game.

Single-mindedness and devotion to a cause are requirements for achieving many difficult goals. But there is one peculiar price a serious athlete must pay, one that scares off many whose talent might otherwise bring them victory. In order to beat a record or an opposing player or team, the athlete must endure and overcome intense physical pain. Don Schollander's description of pain in competitive swimming could serve as a model for nearly all sports:

"You learn the pain in practice and you will know it in every race. As you approach the limit of your endurance, it begins, coming on gradually, hitting your stomach first. Then your arms grow heavy and your legs tighten—thighs first, then knees. You sink lower in the water, as though someone were pushing down on your back. You experience perception changes. The sounds of the pool blend together and become a crashing roar in your ears. The water takes on a pinkish tinge. Your stomach feels as though it's going to fall out—every kick hurts like hell—and then suddenly you hear a shrill, internal scream. . . . It is right there, at the pain barrier, that the great competitors separate from the rest."

From this description one might think that athletes are automatons, intent on winning and numb to pain and other normal human feelings. But the nine people represented in this book show this isn't so. For all their similarities as athletes, they were still individuals: they grew up in widely different times and places, met different problems, and had their own hopes and fears. Each speaks in his or her distinctive voice, describing with humor, pride, or bitterness the rewards and frustrations of breaking into a particular sport.

Each selection has been chosen to focus on a crucial period in an individual's life. At the same time, each reflects some special aspect of the athletic experience. Taken together, the nine accounts give a full and dramatic picture of the serious young athlete's world.

The first three stories reveal the backgrounds and motivations of three young competitors who are just leaving home. Rube Marquard, who grew up in Cleveland at the turn of the century, was so determined to play baseball that he ran away from home at 16. Sixty years later, Spencer Haywood was so eager to get away from Mississippi that he left home at 15. Shortly afterward he discovered that his basketball talent could be a means of permanent escape from his early surroundings. By contrast, Mickey Mantle went away reluctantly to follow his fortune in baseball, and he often wanted desperately to return to his home and family.

The second three stories consider some of the darker aspects of being a serious young athlete. Anthony Quinn, the popular film star, was an aspiring boxer at 15. His story represents a large group of young athletes—those who have great ambitions but never succeed. Dave Meggyesy was a successful pro football player who quit the game at the height of his career. Looking back at his high school days, he was disillusioned about football and its values. Don Schollander succeeded early, becoming a world-champion swimmer at 18. But living up to his role as a champion became his biggest challenge.

The final stories show three athletes who broke into their sports against enormous odds. At 14, Althea Gibson faced an unpromising future as a welfare recipient in Harlem. But in a few years, with the help of many generous supporters, she became a star in the rich man's game of tennis. Hockey player Ted Green was a valuable defenseman for the Boston Bruins when he suffered a terrible injury. He describes the physical and emotional strain of breaking in all over again. The final story recounts Jackie Robinson's early weeks as the first black player in organized baseball, when he faced pressures seldom met by any young person in or out of sport.

These nine athletes were different from us in many ways. They had physical abilities—speed, strength, timing, and grace—that few of us will ever attain. And they had a competitive drive that is rare even among athletes.

But in many ways they were not so different at all. Breaking in is an adventure that nearly everyone faces. Anyone who has moved to a new town, changed schools, or even entered a room of strangers knows the excitement and apprehension in encountering new situations and new people—the same feelings experienced by young athletes in a more dramatic setting. Somewhere in these accounts a reader may find a reflection of his or her own experience, discovering that someone else has passed the same way before. Learning that people in such different circumstances can be so much like us is one of the pleasures in gaining a glimpse into the lives of others.

LAWRENCE T. LORIMER

Breaking In

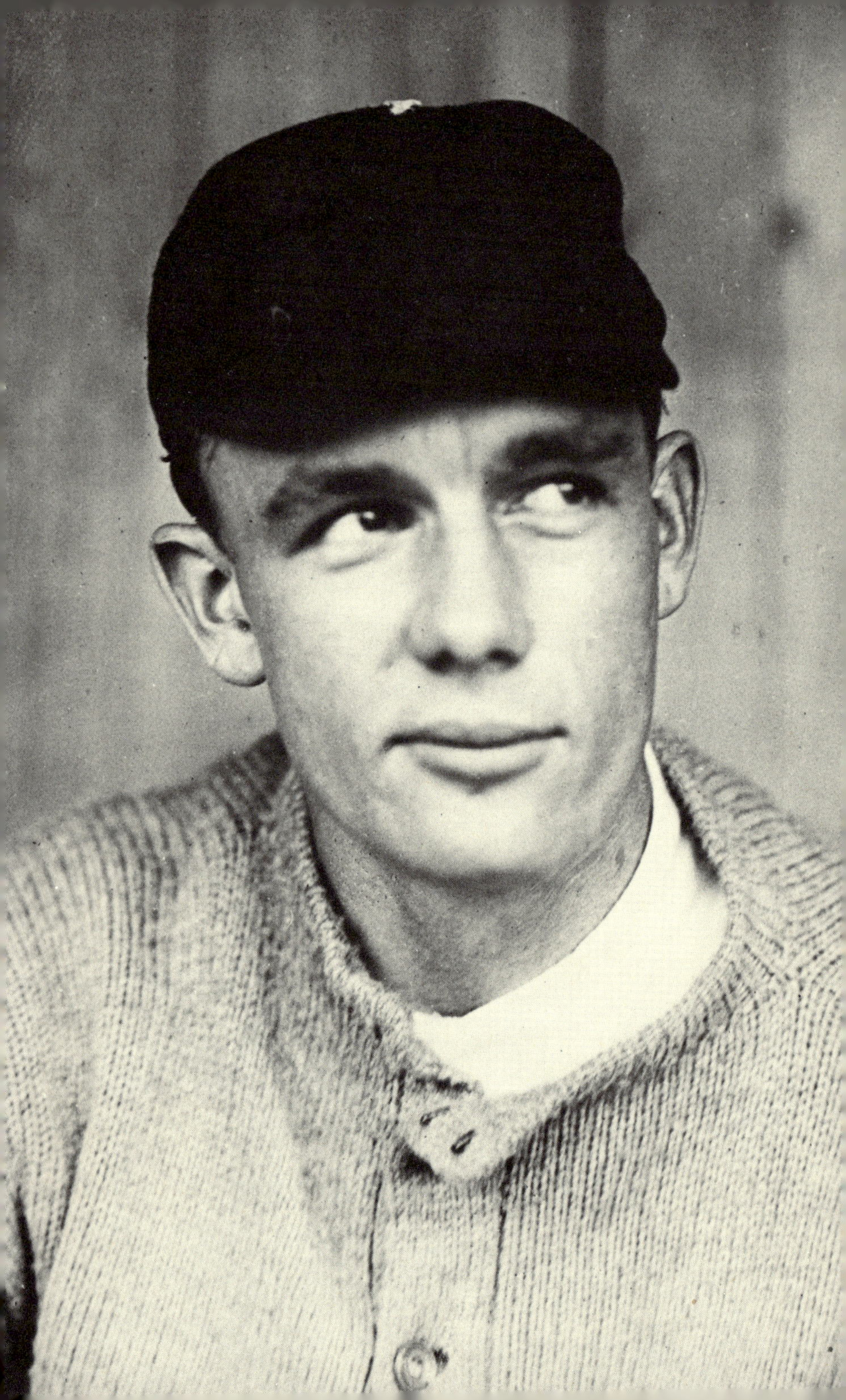

Rube Marquard
I'M GOING TO BE A BALLPLAYER

■For some young people, sport is a hobby. For some it is a part of life that is taken for granted. But for a small number, sport is an obsession.

Rube Marquard was in the last group. When he was barely 16 he knew that he wanted to be a baseball player. Becoming an athlete was not just a dream or an ambition, it was a necessity. And Rube was willing to risk almost anything to follow his star—even the complete disapproval of his father.

Marquard entered baseball in the early years of the century. Both major leagues had been established, and there was a well-organized system of minor leagues. Since radio

Rube Marquard

and television did not exist then, baseball fans had to see their teams play in person or follow their progress in the newspapers. Fans in the horse-and-buggy age were serious about their baseball, and followed their local teams more avidly than they do today.

Yet the more refined citizens of the time considered baseball players uncouth, uneducated, and lazy. Rube's father felt he had good reason to discourage his son from such a disreputable career. But Rube was willing to leave everything behind at 16, and eventually his faith in himself proved justified.

Rube's first hard lesson was that baseball men would take advantage of him if he let them. He learned to insist on being paid what he was worth. His cheerful cockiness was a valuable attitude for a young ballplayer.

Marquard gave the following account of his career many years later when he was an old man, and it appears in Lawrence S. Ritter's great collection of baseball reminiscences, *The Glory of Their Times*. Perhaps some of his experiences were more painful to live through than he remembered years later. But even the greatest stars seldom look back over their lives with so much good humor and satisfaction.

I'M GOING TO BE A BALLPLAYER

My nickname being what it is, you probably automatically assume I must have been a country boy. That's what most people figure. But it's not so. Fact is, my father was the Chief Engineer of the city of Cleveland, and that's where I was born and reared.

Then how come I'm called "Rube"? Well, I'll get to that. But let me tell you about my father first. Like I say, he was the Chief Engineer of the city of Cleveland. As far as he was concerned, the only important thing was for me to get a good education. But as far back as I can remember all I could think of, morning, noon, and night, was baseball.

"Now listen," Dad would say, "I want you to cut this out and pay attention to your studies. I want you to go to college when you're through high school, and I don't want any foolishness about it. Without an education you won't be able to get a good job, and then you'll *never* amount to anything."

"I already have a job," I'd say.

"You've got a job? What are you talking about?"

"I'm going to be a ballplayer."

"A ballplayer?" he'd say, and throw his hands up in the air. "What do you mean? How can you make a living being a ballplayer? I don't understand why a grown man would wear those funny-looking suits in the first place."

"Well," I'd answer, "you see policemen with uniforms on, and other people like that. They change after they're through working. It's the same way with ballplayers."

"Ha! Do ballplayers get paid?"

"Yes, they get paid."

"I don't believe it!"

And round and round we'd go. We'd have exactly the same argument at least once a week. Sometimes my grandfather—my father's father—would get involved in it. He liked baseball and he'd take my side.

"Listen," he'd say to my father, "when you were a youngster I wanted you to be something, too. I wanted you to be a stonecutter, same as I was when I came over from the old country. But no, you wouldn't listen. You wanted to be an engineer. So you became an engineer. Now Richard wants to be a baseball player. He's so determined that nothing is going to stop him. Let's give him a chance and see what he can do."

But Dad would never listen. "Ballplayers are no good," he'd say, "and they never will be any good."

And with that he'd slam the door and go outside and sit on the porch, and not talk to either my grandfather or me for the rest of the evening.

The thing is, I was always very tall for my age. I had three brothers and a sister, and my sister was the shortest of the five of us. She grew to be six feet two. So I was always hanging around the older kids and playing ball with them instead of with kids my own age. When I was about thirteen I used to carry bats for Napoleon Lajoie and Elmer Flick and Terry Turner and a lot of the other Cleveland Indians.

Then later I even pitched a few games for Bill Bradley's Boo Gang. Bill Bradley was the Cleveland third baseman—one of the greatest who ever lived—and he also barnstormed with his Boo Gang after the season was over. So by the time I was only fifteen or sixteen I knew a lot of ballplayers, and I had my heart set on becoming a Big Leaguer myself.

One of my friends was a catcher named Howard Wakefield. He was about five years older than I was. In 1906 he was playing for the Waterloo club in the Iowa State League, and that summer—when I was only sixteen—I got a letter from him.

"We can use a good left-handed pitcher," the letter said, "and if you want to come to Waterloo I'll recommend you to the manager." I think Howard thought that I was at least eighteen or nineteen, because I was so big for my age.

I wrote Howard that my Dad didn't want me to play ball, so I didn't think he'd give me the money to go. If I asked him, he'd probably hit me over the head with something. Except for that, I was ready to go. Now if they could possibly arrange to send me some money for transportation. . . .

Well, pretty soon I got a telegram from the Waterloo

manager. He said: "You've been recommended very highly by Howard Wakefield. I'd like you to come out here and try out with us. If you make good, then we'll reimburse you for your transportation and give you a contract."

Of course, that wasn't much of an improvement over Howard's letter. So I went upstairs to my room and closed the door and wrote back a long letter to the manager, explaining that I didn't have any money for transportation. But if he sent me an advance right now for transportation, then I'd take the next train to Waterloo and he could take it off my salary later on, after I made good. I didn't have the slightest doubt that I would make good. And, of course, I didn't mention that I was only sixteen years old.

I mailed the letter to Iowa, and then I waited on pins and needles for an answer. Every day I had to be the first one to get at the mail, because if anyone else saw a letter to me from the Waterloo ball club that would have been enough to alert Dad to what was going on and I'd have been sunk. So every day I waited for the first sight of the mailman and tried to get to him before he reached the house.

As it turned out, I could have saved myself a lot of worrying. Because no letter ever came. Three weeks passed and still no answer. I couldn't understand what had gone wrong. Maybe it was against the rules to send transportation money to somebody not yet under contract? Maybe they didn't know how good I really was? Maybe this and maybe that.

Finally, I just couldn't stand it anymore. I gave some excuse to my folks about where I was going—like on an overnight camping trip with the Boy Scouts—and I took off for Waterloo, Iowa, on my own.

From Cleveland, Ohio, I bummed my way to Waterloo, Iowa. I was sixteen years old and I'd never been away from home before. It took me five days and five nights, riding freight trains, sleeping in open fields, hitching rides any way I could. My money ran out on the third day, and after that I ate when and how I could.

Finally, though, I arrived at my destination. It was early in the evening of the fifth day. The freight slowly drew into the Illinois Central station at Waterloo, Iowa, and just before it stopped I jumped off and went head over heels right in front of the passenger house. I hardly had time to pick myself up off the ground before the stationmaster grabbed me.

"What do you think you're doing?" he growled. "Come on, get out of here before I run you in."

"No," I said, "I'm reporting to the Waterloo ball club."

"You're what?" he says. "My God, did you ever wash your face?"

"Yes, I did," I said, "but I've been traveling five days and five nights and I'm anxious to get to the ball park. Where do the ballplayers hang around?"

"At the Smoke Shop," he said, "down the street about half a mile. If you walk down there probably whoever you're looking for will be there."

So I thanked him and told him I'd see that he got a free pass to the ball game as soon as I got settled, and started off for the Smoke Shop. It turned out that two brothers owned the Smoke Shop, and they also owned the ball club. One of them was behind the counter when I walked in. He took one look at me and let out a roar.

"What are you doing in here?" he yelled. "This is a respectable place. Get out of here."

"Wait a minute," I said. "I've got a telegram from the manager of the ball club to report here, and if I make good I'll get a contract."

"Are you kidding?" he said. "Who in the world ever recommended you?"

"Howard Wakefield did."

"Well," he said, "Wakefield is in back shooting billiards. We'll soon settle this!"

"I'd like to go back and see him," I said.

"Don't you go back there," he shouted. "You'll drive everybody out. Did you ever take a bath?"

"Of course I did," I said, "but I've bummed my way here and I haven't had a chance to clean up yet."

So he called to the back and in a minute out came Howard. "Holy Cripes!" he said. "What happened to you?"

I was explaining it to him when in came Mr. Frisbee, the manager, and I was introduced to him. "I received your telegram," I said. "I didn't have enough money to come first class or anything like that, but here I am."

"Keokuk is here tomorrow," he said, "and we'll pitch you."

"Tomorrow? You don't want me to pitch tomorrow, after what I've been through?"

"Tomorrow or never, young fellow!"

"All right," I said. "But could I have $5 in advance so I can get a clean shirt or something?"

"After the game tomorrow," he said, and walked away.

So Howard took me to his rooming house, and I cleaned up there and had something to eat, and they let me sleep on an extra cot they had.

The next day we went out to the ball park and I was introduced to the players and given a uniform that was too small for me. The Keokuk team was shagging balls while I warmed up, and they kept making comments about green rookies and bushers and how they'd knock me out of the box in the first inning. Oh, I felt terrible. I had an awful headache and I was exhausted. But I was determined to show them that I could make good, and I went out there and won that game, 6-1.

With that I felt sure I'd be offered a contract. So after the game I went to Mr. Frisbee and said, "Well, I showed you I could deliver the goods. Can we talk about a contract now?"

"Oh," he said, "Keokuk is in last place. Wait until Oskaloosa comes in this weekend. They're in second place.

They're a tough team, and if you can beat them then we'll talk."

"Can't I get any money, any advance money, on my contract?" I asked him.

"You haven't got a contract," he said.

"All right," I said, and I didn't say another word.

That evening I didn't say anything to anybody. But when it got dark I went down to the railroad station, and the same stationmaster was there.

"Hey," he said, "you pitched a fine game today. I was there and you did a great job. What are you doing back here? Did you come to give me that free ticket you promised me?"

"No, I'm sorry," I said. "I'm going back home to Cleveland, and I want to know what time a freight comes by." And I explained to him everything that had happened.

He was very nice to me, and after we talked awhile he said, "Look, this train comes in at one o'clock in the morning and the engine unhooks and goes down to the water tower. When it does, you sneak into the baggage compartment, and meanwhile I'll talk to the baggage man before the engine gets hooked up again. Then when the train pulls out and is about five miles out of town he'll open the baggage door and let you out."

So that all happened, and when we were five miles out of town the door opened and the baggage man appeared. I talked with him all the way to Chicago, and as we got close to the yards he said to me, "OK, you better get ready to jump now. There are a lot of detectives around here and if you're not careful they'll grab you and throw you in jail. So once you get on the ground, don't hesitate. Beat it away from here as fast as you can."

The baggage man must have told the engineer about me, because we slowed down to a crawl just before we approached the Chicago yards, and off I jumped. I got out of there quick and took off down the street. I don't know what street it was, and I'm not sure where I was headed, but I do remember that I was awfully tired. It was the middle of the morning and I had hardly slept a wink the night before.

I'd walked about three or four blocks when I passed by a fire engine house. Evidently all the firemen were out at a fire, because the place was empty. I was tired, so I went in and sat down. Well, they had a big-bellied iron stove in there, and it was warm, and I guess I must have fallen asleep, because the next thing I knew a couple of firemen were shaking me and doing everything they could to wake me up. They called me a bum and a lot of other names, and told me to get out of there or they'd have me thrown in jail.

"I'm no bum," I said, "I'm a ballplayer."

"What, you a ballplayer! Where did you ever play?"

So I told them: Cleveland, around the sandlots, and in Waterloo, Iowa, too. And I told them all about it.

They still didn't really believe me. They asked me did I know Three-Fingered Brown, Tinker, Evers, Chance, and all those fellows.

"No," I said, "I don't know them. But some day I'll be playing with them, or against them, because I'm going to get in the Big Leagues."

"Where are you going now?" they asked me.

"Back home to Cleveland."

"Have you got any money?"

"No."

So they got up a little pool of about $5 and said, "Well, on your way. And use this to get something to eat."

I thanked them, and as I left I told them that some day I'd be back. "When I get to the Big Leagues," I said, "I'm coming out to visit you when we get to Chicago."

■Marquard went home to Cleveland. The next summer he got a job with an ice cream company, checking ice cream shipments during the week and pitching for the company team on Sundays. He received $25 a week.

Then one day he got a card from the Cleveland Indians inviting him to come to their office to discuss a contract. When he arrived, officials offered him $100 a month, less than he was making. Others would have jumped at any major league offer—but not Marquard, especially after his experience at Waterloo. When the Indians would not increase the offer, the 17-year-old pitcher walked out.

On his way home he stopped at a sporting goods store where baseball people hung out and told them what had happened. One of his listeners was Charlie Carr, the manager of the Indianapolis team in the minor league American Association. Carr asked Marquard how much money he wanted and Marquard boldly said $200 a month. Carr agreed to the demand, and Marquard signed an agreement with Indianapolis on the spot.

When I got home that night I had to tell my Dad about it, because I was to leave for Indianapolis the next day. Oh, that was a terrible night. Finally, Dad said, "Now listen, I've told you time and time again that I don't want you to be a professional ballplayer. But you've got your mind made up. Now I'm going to tell you something: when you cross that threshold, don't come back. I don't ever want to see you again."

"You don't mean that, Dad," I said.

"Yes, I do."

"Well, I'm going," I said, "and some day you'll be proud of me."

"Proud!" he said. "You're breaking my heart, and I don't ever want to see you again."

"I won't break your heart," I said. "I'll add more years to your life. You wait and see."

So I went to Indianapolis. They optioned me out to Canton in the Central League for the rest of the 1907 season, and I won 23 games with them, which was one-third of all the games the Canton club won that year.

Next year—that would be 1908—I went to spring

training with the Indianapolis club. We went to French Lick Springs, Indiana. After three weeks there we went back to Indianapolis and played a few exhibition games before the season opened. Well, believe it or not, the first club to come in for an exhibition game was the Cleveland team: Napoleon Lajoie, Terry Turner, Elmer Flick, George Stovall, and the whole bunch that I used to carry bats for. When they came on the field I was already warming up.

"Hey, what are you doing here?" a couple of them yelled at me. "Are you the bat boy here?"

"No," I said, "I'm a pitcher."

"You, a pitcher? Who do you think you're kidding?"

"You'll see, I'm going to pitch against you guys today, and I'm going to beat you, too."

"Beat us! Busher, you couldn't beat a drum!"

Well, I pitched the whole nine innings and beat them, 2-0. Lajoie got two hits off me, and I think George Stovall got a couple, but I shut them out.

On opening day Kansas City was at Indianapolis, and I pitched the opening game. I won, 2-1, and that evening the story in the Indianapolis *Star* read like this: "We have a left-hander with Indianapolis who is going places, too. He resembles one of the great left-handed pitchers of all time: Rube Waddell." And from that day on they nicknamed me "Rube."

I had a wonderful season that year with Indianapolis. I pitched 47 complete games, won 28 of them, led the league in most strikeouts, least hits, most innings pitched, and everything. Occasionally what I'd do would be reported in the Cleveland papers, and friends of mine would tell me that they'd pass by the house and see Dad sitting on the porch.

"Well, Fred," they'd say—that was my Dad's name, Fred—"did you see what your son Rube did yesterday?"

"Who are you talking about?" he'd say. "Rube who?"

"Your son, Richard."

"I told him baseball was no good," my Dad would reply. "Now they've even gone and changed his name!"

Late in the season we went into Columbus, Ohio, and Charlie Carr came up to me before the game.

"Rube," he said, "there are going to be an awful lot of celebrities here at the game today. The American and National Leagues both have an off-day, and they're all coming to see you pitch. If you pitch a good game I may be able to sell you before the night is out."

I went out there that day and I pitched one of those unusual games: no hits, no runs, no errors. Twenty-seven men faced me and not one of them got to first base. And that evening in Columbus they put me up for sale, with all the Big-League clubs bidding on me, like a horse being auctioned off. The Cleveland club went as high as $10,500 for my contract, but the Giants went to $11,000, and I was sold to them. At that time that was the highest price ever paid for a baseball player.

18 ■ I'M GOING TO BE A BALLPLAYER

I reported to the New York Giants in September of 1908, as soon as the American Association season was over. I was eighteen years old and I was in the Big Leagues!

I came up too late in the season to make a trip to Chicago with the Giants that year, but the next season we made our first trip to Chicago the second week in June. And the first thing I did, as soon as I got there, was to make a beeline for that firehouse.

The only one there when I first got there was the lieutenant. I walked up to him and said, "Lieutenant, do you remember me?"

"Never saw you before in my life," he said.

"Well, remember about three years ago you caught me sleeping back of that stove there?"

"Oh, are you the kid from Cleveland that said he's a ballplayer?"

"Yes. Remember me? My name is Marquard, Richard Marquard."

"Of course. What are you doing here?"

"I'm in the Big Leagues," I said. "I told you when I got to the Big Leagues I was coming out to visit you."

"Well, I'll be darned," he said. "Who are you with?"

"Why, I'm with the New York Giants."

And boy, for years after that, whenever the Giants would come to Chicago I'd go out to that firehouse. I'd sit out front

New York Giant Rube Marquard warming up.

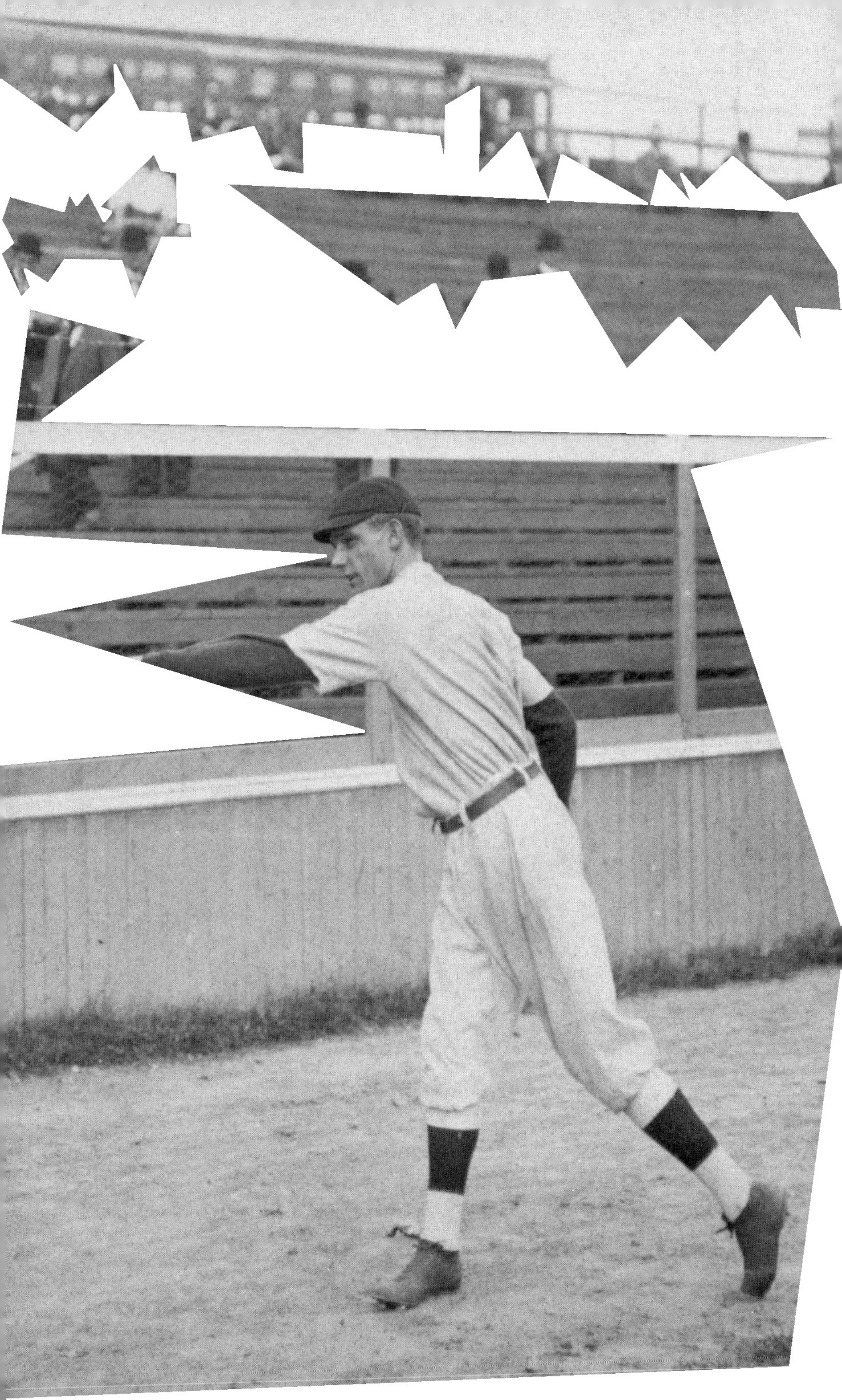

and talk for hours. The firemen would have all the kids in the neighborhood there . . . and all the families that lived around would stop by . . . and it was really wonderful. Everybody was so nice and friendly. Gee, I used to enjoy that. It was a great thrill for me.

■Rube soon became a star for the Giants. In 1911, when he was only 21, he won 25 games. In 1912 he won his first 19 in a row (still a record) and 27 for the season. Then he pitched two World Series victories.

By 1915, however, Rube and John McGraw, the great Giant manager, were feuding. Rube asked to be traded, and McGraw replied that no one would pay anything for him. Rube asked what price McGraw would accept. McGraw said $7,500. As cocky as ever, Marquard called the Brooklyn Dodger manager on the telephone and made a deal—he traded himself to the Dodgers.

Rube had some good years with Brooklyn, helping them win pennants in 1916 and 1920. By the time he left baseball in 1925, he had won 205 games and was recognized as one of the great pitchers of the era. The closing scene of his story occurred during one of his successful years with Brooklyn.

One day when I was pitching for Brooklyn I pitched the first game of a double-header against Boston and beat them, 1-0. I was in the clubhouse during the second game, taking off my uniform, when the clubhouse boy came in.

"Rube," he said, "there's an elderly gentleman outside

who wants to see you. He says he's your father from Cleveland."

"He's not my father," I said. "My father wouldn't go across the street to see me. But you go out and get his autograph book and bring it in, and I'll autograph it for him."

But instead of bringing in the book, he brought in my Dad. And we were both delighted to see one another.

"Boy, you sure are a hardhead," he said to me. "You know I didn't mean what I said ten years ago."

"What about you, Dad?" I said. "You're as stubborn as I am. I thought you never wanted to see me again. I thought you meant it."

"Of course I didn't," he said.

After we talked a while, I said, "Did you see the game today?"

"Yes, I did," he said.

"Where were you sitting?" I asked him.

"Well, you know the man who wears that funny thing on his face?"

"You mean the mask? The catcher?"

"I guess so. Well, anyway, I was halfway between him and the number one—you know, where they run right after they hit the ball."

"You mean first base?"

"I don't know," he said. "I don't know what they call it. I was sitting in the middle there."

"How many ball games have you seen since I became a ballplayer, Dad?"

"This is the first one," he said.

Well, he stayed in New York with me for a few weeks, and we had a great time. Finally, he had to go back to Cleveland. After he'd left, the newspapers heard about my Dad and they wanted to know his address back home. So I gave it to them, and doggone if they didn't send reporters and photographers to Cleveland to interview him.

They took his picture and asked him a lot of questions. One of the things they asked him was whether he had ever played very much baseball himself.

"Oh, of course I did, when I was younger," he told them. "I used to love to play baseball. I used to be a pitcher, just like my son Richard—I mean like my son Rube."

"Are you proud of your son?" they asked him.

"I certainly am," Dad said. "Why shouldn't I be? He's a great baseball player, isn't he?"

Spencer Haywood
IT WAS MY WAY OUT

■Professional sports have traditionally been a way for the poor to move up and out of poverty. In earlier times, American sports heroes were often Irish-Americans, Italian-Americans, and other members of European minorities from big-city slums. Others were farm kids from backward rural parts of the country. In recent years many black athletes from city ghettoes and from the rural Deep South have become stars in nearly all major sports.

Spencer Haywood is one of these black athletes. He was born in Silver City, Mississippi, in 1949, the ninth of eleven children. He left home to go north in his early teens, and by the time he turned 20, he was a nationally known basketball star. Three years later, when he was earning more than

24 ■ IT WAS MY WAY OUT

$200,000 a year with the Seattle SuperSonics, he collaborated with writer Bill Libby on a book about his still new career. It was called *Stand Up for Something,* and in it Haywood told of his early years.

Rube Marquard's obsession had been baseball. Haywood's was escape—from the poverty and hopelessness of his childhood in Mississippi. Before he really discovered his basketball talent, he had fled the South in favor of the streets of Chicago's black ghetto. Once he saw that he could play the game, he knew that basketball must be his means of escape to a better life.

Like many athletes from poor backgrounds, Spencer lacked education and sophistication, and was in danger of being used by ambitious coaches and team owners. But he more than made up for these deficiencies with his talent and his intense desire to succeed. In fact, he was willing to use coaches and team owners to achieve his own ambitions.

Young athletes from many backgrounds seek the money and respect that success in sports can bring. But those from poor and disadvantaged homes are hungrier—they have more to gain by succeeding and more to lose if they fail. Their great drive is far less common among athletes from more comfortable homes.

In this excerpt Haywood recalls his childhood in Mississippi, his days in Chicago, and his early basketball successes. His account lacks the good humor of Marquard's story—

Spencer Haywood at the University of Detroit.

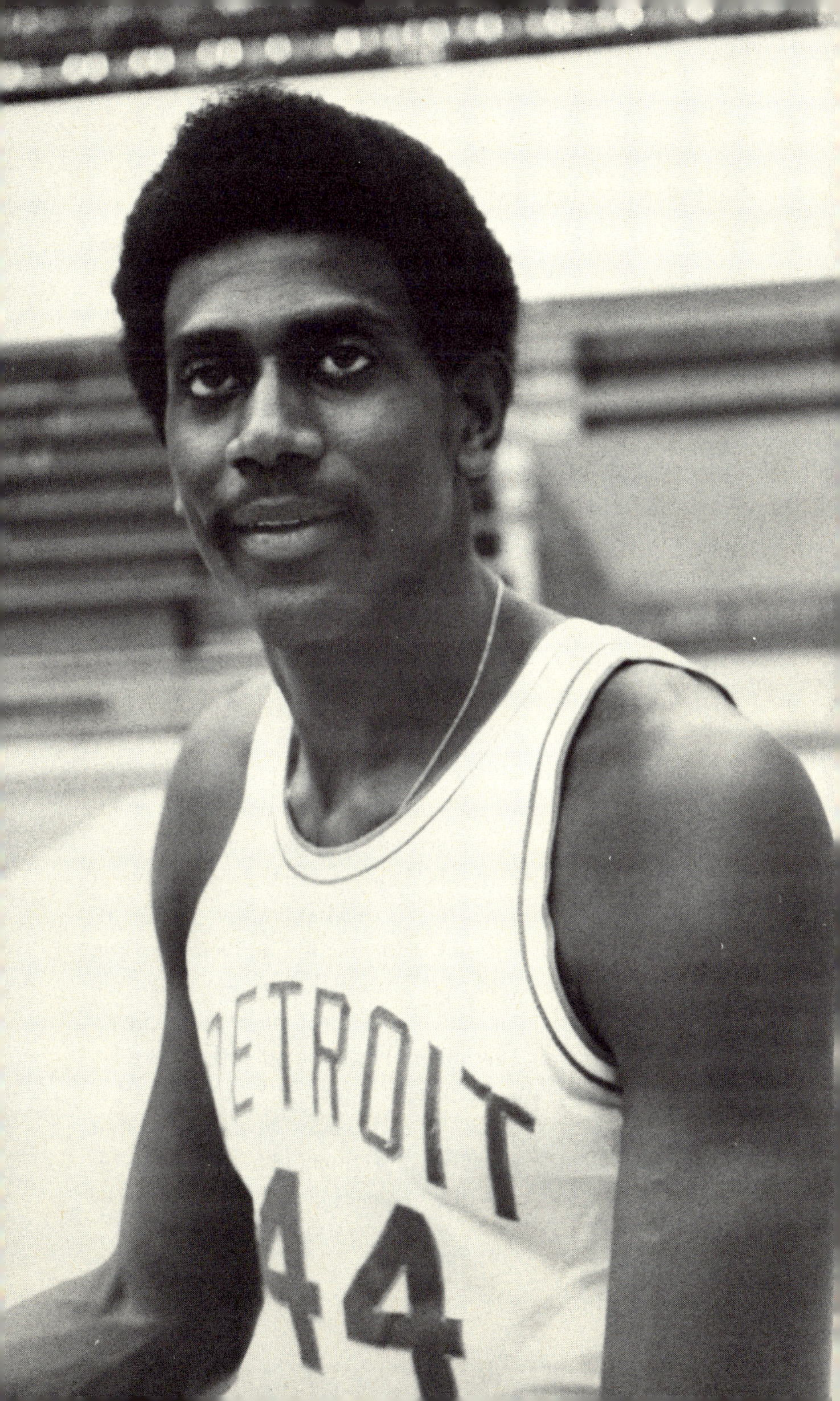
DETROIT
44

Spencer's hard work and humiliations are still too fresh in his mind to be taken lightly. He begins his story by describing his life in Silver City, Mississippi.

IT WAS MY WAY OUT

The rules were different for people like us in a place like that. We just lived. You had babies and you worked and you tried to survive. When you got old enough to get out, you got out. Except the mamas and the papas who have to stay to take care of the kids. Except they didn't always stay. You don't admire a man or a woman for running out on his family, but you can understand it when gettin' out is as important as it is there. My daddy got out: he died. I don't know what he died of. In places like that, people like us don't know. You get sick and you live or you die. You seldom see a doctor. I was born at home, delivered by a midwife, a neighbor lady. Sometimes there the mamas deliver their babies by themselves. And then they care for them until they are old enough to get out.

My daddy was only in his early sixties when he died, but he was probably best off out of it. It would have been better for us if he'd lived because he could of made a living for us as a carpenter and after he died it was hard for my mama to take care of us. As I was growing up, the older kids began to leave to go north, but there still was a mess of us Haywoods to take care of. We didn't have much. We had our house, but we had to pay taxes on it. Daddy built it, and he probably did the best he could with what he had, but it wasn't much, and we wore it out living in it. It was six rooms, I think, just a big old raggedy house, wood frame, paint peeling, holes in the floor.

We slept three to a bed. Growing up that way was bad because it seemed like the younger one always got the middle and he was always peein' in the bed and the others were always getting peed on and wet and disgusted and yellin' for ma, though there wasn't much she could do about it. It was hot in the summer and cold in the winter. I mean sweatin' hot and freezin' cold. We had no gas. We had a wood stove. And a wood heater which would go out in the middle of the night. We'd take turns getting up at five or six in the morning to go outside into the cold winters to chop wood so there'd be a fire goin' in the heater and a little heat in the house when the others woke up and so there was some wood in the stove so mama could cook some mush or something for breakfast for us.

We didn't always have enough to eat. We were hungry a lot. The worst thing was going to bed hungry. It hurt in your gut. You curled up in pain and it was awful. You prayed just to fall asleep. The only thing worse was waking up hungry and knowing there wasn't any food to take that hunger from you. And we didn't have the clothes to keep us warm. I had some old raggedy levis and some old raggedy shirts. I was seven years old before I got my first pair of shoes. I had been going to school for a year. To this day my toes curl under. Salvation Army shoes did that. They were too small. I never had a suit of clothes until I was up north and almost out of high school. When I was growing up, I wore hand-me-downs and clothes my mama could get from the Salvation Army. And I used to write my brothers up north for clothes.

Mama made around $10 a week scrubbing floors and such and she got around $10 a week relief money. That was most of what we had to live on. Mama would go out and wash floors and come home with a little bag of groceries. As soon as we could, we all went out and worked to help out. We started at six or seven, in the fields, mowing lawns, caddying. I started at six, before I had shoes. But there wasn't much for us. We couldn't make much. Those that had gone north sent money home sometimes, but not often. They didn't have to send. And mama would never ask. I picked cotton, did anything for a few pennies. And when I got it, I gave it to mama. A candy bar was a luxury I never knew.

We were poor. We were super-poor. When you don't have anything, you are as poor as you can be. You don't get any poorer than we were. And I knew it, even then. Hell, man, you could see others who had more. All you needed was eyes in your head. We saw how the white folks lived—nice houses, nice cars, nice clothes, food on the table, television sets, money to go to the movies. Even the poor whites had more than we did. It's hard not to hate whites in a situation like that. Hell, when you've got nothing, you hate anyone who has more.

Mama musta seen how it really was, but she never complained. I remember her crying, though. She was tremendously strong. She was tough. She had no hatred in her. She just knew what had to be done, and she did it. She had no education. She never thought about how hard it was. She just did it. But every once in a while it must have gotten to be too much for her, her kids not having shoes or enough clothes to wear or enough food to eat. And she'd get tired, I guess. She had bad legs and they'd hurt her. And I remember once in a while her sittin' down and just crying. She didn't like for us to see her cry. She wanted to be strong for us, to make us strong. But sometimes it just got to be too much for her.

She used to say she wished we could have some toys like kids like to have. I never had a Christmas present until I was 16 years old and living with some other people up north. It was all mama could do to scuffle around and get together a Christmas turkey dinner for us. Somehow she always managed. But then we'd go hungry for a month to make up for it. And there was never anything left over for presents. I never had a toy in my life.

We found some fun. We swam in old mud holes. We played golf with broken sticks on a course we made up out back of our crib. We played basketball, but we never had a basketball. We nailed up an old rusty hoop. And we threw tin cans at it. Or we stuffed socks to make a ball. We pretended to dribble by saying "Bop, bop." You was allowed two "bops," then you had to shoot or pass off.

I started out at McNair High School. It was an all-black school and you couldn't get a decent education there. When I was 14, 15 years old I had maybe a third-grade education. I could hardly read or write. I wasn't thinking of finishing school. You don't in a place like that. There is no point to it. I wasn't even thinking of going to college through basketball. It just didn't occur to me. In a place like that, you're hardly even scouted.

The first year I played, I made the varsity, but I wasn't any good. I was damn good at shooting socks and tin cans, but not basketballs. There were older guys ahead of me, and I was just an extra man. And there weren't enough uniforms to go around. The school colors were green and yellow, and the others would go out in green and I'd go out in yellow. That was one of the worst years of my life. You have to know what it is to be in yellow when the others are in green. They'd put me in in the last minute or two of one-sided games and I couldn't even make a layup. The second year I began to come on. I got a regular uniform and I made the regular team. I averaged 15, 16 points a game. The coach was Charles Wilson and he was all right. But there wasn't much competition and I doubt if I'd have developed much if I'd have stayed there. I wasn't going to stay, anyway, I was going to get out if it killed me.

When I was 14, my brother Joe and sister Lena came back to visit at Christmas. I took one look at their car and I said, "Wow! Joe's made it." I begged them to take me back north with them, to Chicago where they lived. I didn't know what was there. They didn't tell me nothing about life in a ghetto. I figured it had to be better than *this*. I just wanted to see it. But mama said I was too young. I wouldn't give up on it. I hung around their car for days scared to death they'd sneak out on me. When they said they were going, I locked myself in the car and I wouldn't get out. I screamed and cried. Mama hauled me out of that car and beat hell out of me. But I wouldn't let up. "Just for a visit," I said. "Just for a little while." I begged and I cried. Finally they agreed. On condition I was sent back the next week. I stayed a month. And the minute I got home I started plotting to go back. I worked in the fields and on the golf course and sold empty pop bottles and I saved my money and the day school let out the next summer I was on the bus on my way back to Chicago.

I moved in with Lena and her husband, Clarence. They were good to me. But they didn't have much for me. And they had their things to do. It was "I got a key, you got a key." So I did my own things. I was on my own. I was only 15, but I was big for my age. Tall, of course. I lied about my age and got a job washing dishes at the Fred Harvey restaurant. I made sixty bucks a week. I got by.

The moment I got to Chicago I saw what it was. A ghetto. Filthy streets. Rat-infested tenements. People living in rat-traps. People living on welfare. People without hope. But it was better than any life I'd known. It was better than being beat down in the south, you see. And I wasn't ever goin' back to live in Mississippi. No way. Not ever.

I got an education on the streets of Chicago and later in Detroit. By the time I was 16, 17 years old I knew things some people who don't live in the ghettoes will never know. Both places I found out about pimps and prostitutes and pushers and junkies and thieves. The streets was full of 'em. Whatever they were, they were your people, brothers and sisters. Hell, pimps and pushers are people a poor boy looks up to in a place like that. They got the big cars and the fancy clothes and the pretty ladies and the roll of bills. Hell, they made it. It doesn't matter how they got it. You know no one's giving them anything. So if they got it, that's groovy, that's cool.

We had gang fights. We fought each other. But mostly we beat up on whites. I learned to use my fists. I learned to be tough. You got to, to survive. If you're scared, you don't let on. I stole. I carried a .22 in my pocket, snatched purses, and mugged Whitey. We'd steal from stores for food. We'd case a place, see where the people went, and slip in and stuff some stuff in our shirts and slip out. Maybe someone would raise a little hell in some other part of the store while we did our thing. I was just lucky I was never caught. I never was sent away. I never served time. I never graduated to big stuff. Friends who were with me there then in those places did. Some of them are in stir. Some of them are shot to death. You don't think of them as bad. I don't. Sure, what they did was bad, but you don't think of it that way. The way you think of it is they was unlucky, they got caught. If you can't sing a song, man, or stuff a basketball, or something like that, you got to find some way.

I started drinking wine when I was 14 years old. I drank other stuff, but wine was cheapest, so wine it was. I smoked pot, whenever I could get my hands on some. I took some pills. And sniffed heroin. I just never got hooked.

Basketball saved me from becoming an alky or an addict or a hood. When I got into it, I could see it was the way out for me. Someone would say to me, "Hey, man, you should try this." And I'd say, "No, man, I been down that road. My thing is basketball. I can't afford to mess with that crap." And they'd act hurt, like I'd put 'em down or offended 'em. And it'd make me feel bad. Like, you want to be with 'em. But you got to be hard. My best friend was hooked and I could see myself through him and what I'd be, and I didn't want that for me. And I had a goal. You get a goal, you got to go for it.

■Haywood started playing serious basketball on the playgrounds of Chicago. He was only 15 years old, but big-city playground ball could develop a young man's talent in a hurry. He could watch such future stars as Cazzie Russell and Dave Bing, and might even get to play with them.

At the end of Spencer's summer in Chicago, his older brother Roy came to visit. Roy was on a basketball scholarship at Bowling Green University in Ohio. He came out to a playground to watch Spencer play.

"People tell me you're good," Roy said.

I said, "I'm not bad." I didn't know if I was good or bad. I took him on, one-on-one. I held my own.

He said, "Hell, you can play." He said I should go back to Bowling Green with him and he'd fix it up for me so I could play high school ball around there. He figured I had a chance to make it, and he wanted to help me get it. I said, "Sure." So I packed up my one suitcase and took off with him for Ohio.

I played ball with Roy and some of the other players who were hanging around school in the gym. And the guys said, "Hey, kid, you can play this game." And I began to believe I could. And I began to play like it. And some of the coaches watched and they said, "Hey, this guy's gonna be good," and they wanted me to go to high school near there so they could get me into their college when the time came.

I was around 6-6 then and I could jump and I had good

hands and I'd been learning the game fast from good players. No coaching, but learning from players. Just doing it. And getting better. And seeing how impressed people were. And beginning to be impressed with myself. And it was then for the first time that I really started thinking of maybe getting to go to college so I could become a pro. I'd probably never even have gone back to high school if it hadn't been for basketball. But everyone was saying, "Hey, man, this dude's gonna do it," so I began to think maybe.

But it didn't work out at Bowling Green. Roy couldn't find any place for me to stay, and he couldn't handle me himself. Anyway, he had this idea in the back of his head all along that he'd take me to Will Robinson, who was the coach at Pershing High in Detroit. Roy hadn't played for Will, but he'd played against Will's teams and he knew Will had super-teams and turned out super-players he sent to college and some to pro ball. And Roy knew from his reputation that Will sometimes helped kids like me. Well, Roy took me to Will, and I guess Will saw me for a player, because he fixed me up right away.

He sort of took to me right off, too, I think, because he became my guardian. Then Will found me a home with James and Ida Bell, who became my joint guardians with Will. Mr. Bell was a foreman at the Chrysler plant in Detroit and made a nice living and they had a nice home. They had two sons about my age, Greg and James, but the Bells accepted me as another son and their sons accepted me as a brother and I just started living there like it was my home.

I was used to the streets and life on the streets and drinking and sexing and fixing and I sneaked around some for awhile. But the Bells and Will Robinson straightened me out. They treated me like a son. One Christmas, they gave me my first present—a sweater. They gave me love, so I had to respect them. They kept after me until I straightened myself out. They showed me how I was getting a chance and would be a fool to blow it. They saw to it that I didn't want for anything. They stressed studies. Pershing was a beautiful school. Black and white, but no black-white troubles. No hassle. You could get a good education there. It wasn't a disgrace. And you could play ball there. And Will Robinson made me see for sure I had a future in basketball. For the first time, I had a future.

Robinson was a good coach. He knew the game inside out and he was tough. He didn't take any nonsense from his kids. If you wanted to play for him, you played his way. And everyone wanted to play for him because he turned out good players. Mel Daniels, for example, came just before me. Ira Harge, another ABA star, came just before me, too.

When practice started, we climbed ropes, did push-ups, sit-ups, ran all day for two or three weeks. We never played a lick. When everyone was dead, then was when he threw the ball out there. Then was when we first started scrimmaging. And we had hard scrimmages. All-out. With the emphasis on fundamentals. I thought I was a pretty good player, but he was climbing all over my butt all the time. He wasn't going to play me for any favorite.

At first, I got fed up fast. I wasn't used to it. My tail was dragging and my spirit was shot. I figured, who needs it? It was my future, sure, but there are times a kid doesn't look around the corner. I called up my brother and complained. I was ready to quit. I wanted out. I was happier on the streets. He talked me into sticking with it. I knew I should. I just needed someone to say I should.

It got better. I got in better shape, I got to know what I was doing and what was expected of me, and I got used to Robinson. I liked the school and the school began to like me when they saw what I could do in basketball. I began to hit the books some and I began to do better in my studies. I had a D average my first year, a C average my second year, and a B average my third year. That's not bad when you realize I was illiterate going in. I could hardly read and I couldn't write legibly and I couldn't talk decent because I didn't know all the words. I began to gain confidence in myself as a person. The Bells were beautiful to me, and so was Will. I began to feel like I had a place in life.

The basketball couldn't have been better. Robinson had a style of play with running and movement and shooting that a guy could carry over into college and pro ball. We were in shape and we were prepared. And we had good players. In my junior year, we didn't lose much, but we did lose out on the titles. In my senior year we lost only one game, by one point. We wound up beating Pontiac Central in the state finals in East Lansing at Michigan State University fieldhouse.

■By this time Haywood was 6-foot-8 and weighed 215 pounds. He was a great jumper and had a beautiful soft shot. Although his grades were improving, he was scarcely ready for college work. Yet almost every major college coach in the country was interested in him.

Will Robinson served as Spencer's buffer, forcing the college people to speak to him first. By Robinson's count, some 335 colleges contacted him about Spencer. Some recruiters sent letters or telegrams, some telephoned, and many came to Detroit, trying to talk to Spencer in person.

He took a load off my shoulders, but a lot of people got to me anyway. I know I had offers from every Big Ten school, including Michigan, of course. I had offers from Detroit, of course, and from Bowling Green, my brother's school. I had offers from a lot of Far West schools, including UCLA and USC and the Air Force Academy. I had offers from a lot of Southeastern and Southwestern schools. I'm sure some didn't know I was black and some were so interested in getting a good player they wouldn't have cared if he was purple. Most of the offers were legit, though some were shady. Some hinted I could get money under the table for pretending to work at jobs, cars, all the clothes I needed, even ladies. Few of them said much about my studies. I suppose they supposed I wasn't interested.

It turned my head, some. You know, man, here I was just learning to learn and some of the biggest-name colleges in the country wanted me because I could play basketball. It gave me a sense of power I'd never had before. It gave me a feeling of independence. Robinson was trying to give me advice, but I was wanting to go my own way. At first I wanted to go to the Air Force because it seemed funny to think of myself as a fly-boy. Then I wanted to go to UCLA because I liked the idea of playing with Big Lew [Alcindor, later known as Kareem Abdul-Jabbar]. But then I got to thinking about being in Alcindor's shadow and I forgot about that.

I finally decided to go to Tennessee. That sounds crazy, I know, and Robinson was dead against it. He figured they just wanted to use me, and he was probably right. But I had met a chick in Knoxville when they brought me to the campus for a visit and I really dug this sister; and even though there sure weren't many blacks in school, there were a lot of them in town, and a lot of sisters I thought I could deal with in the black part of town, and I thought I'd have fun there. It's just a chancy thing, you know, why a guy makes up his mind that he likes this place or that place or wants to go here or there, and a sympathetic sister is as good a reason as any.

But Spencer never played at Tennessee; he flunked the entrance exam. Finally, with the help of the coach at the University of New Mexico, he enrolled at Trinidad Junior College in Colorado. (The New Mexico coach hoped that after a year or two in junior college, Spencer would transfer to his school.) As a freshman, Spencer did well in his studies and was elected to the Junior College All-America team.

The following summer he got his big chance. Most of the top black college stars were boycotting the tryouts for the 1968 U.S. Olympic team because of their disagreement with the racial policies of the International Olympic Committee. As a result, junior college stars were invited to the tryouts. Spencer made the team, becoming the youngest U.S. Olympic basketball player ever. He was 19.

The Olympics were a great triumph for Spencer. Although he was the youngest man on the team, he soon became its star.

After the Olympics some people criticized Spencer for not taking part in the boycott of the Olympic tryouts. But the issues involved in the boycott were distant to him. Some years later Spencer explained his attitude when he described his Olympic experiences in his book.

I know some of the brothers backed out. I suppose I sympathized with some of their sentiments. But I wasn't any part of that. They didn't let me in on it. No one spoke to me about it. When I was invited to take part in the Olympic trials, it was an opportunity I never dreamed of getting.

Man, there was no way I wanted to pass that up.

Even though some of the big-name ballplayers had pulled out, we had some good talent at the trials and we got some good guys going, like Jo Jo White and Charlie Scott, who are top pros now. I found out I could play with them, and by then I was beginning to feel I could play with anyone. At first, just making the team was a thrill, but then I saw it was my place to lead it so I just took on that responsibility and did it. Hank Iba was the coach, slowdown style, but I just did my thing his way.

We stressed team play and defense and a disciplined offense, which was good because we didn't get to play together long and had to go a little cautious. I gained a lot of confidence on the pre-Olympic tour we took around the country, but when we got to Mexico City I felt unsure of myself at first. I'd never been to a foreign country before and I wasn't used to a lot of different kinds of people being around speaking a lot of different languages and I'd never played before the kind of crowds we played in front of.

I'd get so nervous before games I'd start shaking in the locker room. A couple of times I stumbled running out on the court. All that was expected of us was to win every game and not ever lose even one because no U.S. team ever had. Yet people kept saying we were the worst U.S. team ever and were bound to lose, which fired us up. We were determined to prove we were better than people thought we were. And no one wants to be the first to lose, you know.

Once we began playing, we began winning and it was all right.

When we won the final and took the victory stand and they draped those gold medals around our necks and played the national anthem, it sent shivers down my spine. I mean I'm no super-patriot. I know a lot that's wrong with this country. But, it was the situation. Here I was, 19 years old, the youngest guy ever to play on an American basketball team in the Olympics, the star of the game, how many years out of Mississippi? And all those people from all those other countries who always started out rooting against us because we were the big guys they wanted to see knocked off wound up cheering us. It was some kind of feeling. I don't know where my gold medal is. I don't have a trophy case. I don't even keep many trophies. It wasn't the medal. It wasn't the anthem. It was winning. It was doing that thing.

■Haywood was the big winner in Olympic basketball. Suddenly the player from obscure Trinidad Junior College was a celebrity, and basketball experts around the country knew he would one day be a pro star.

The coach at the University of New Mexico, who had helped Spencer get into Trinidad, hoped he would now transfer to New Mexico. But Spencer enrolled instead at the University of Detroit at the urging of his old high school coach, Will Robinson.

Haywood goes up for a rebound at the 1968 Olympics.

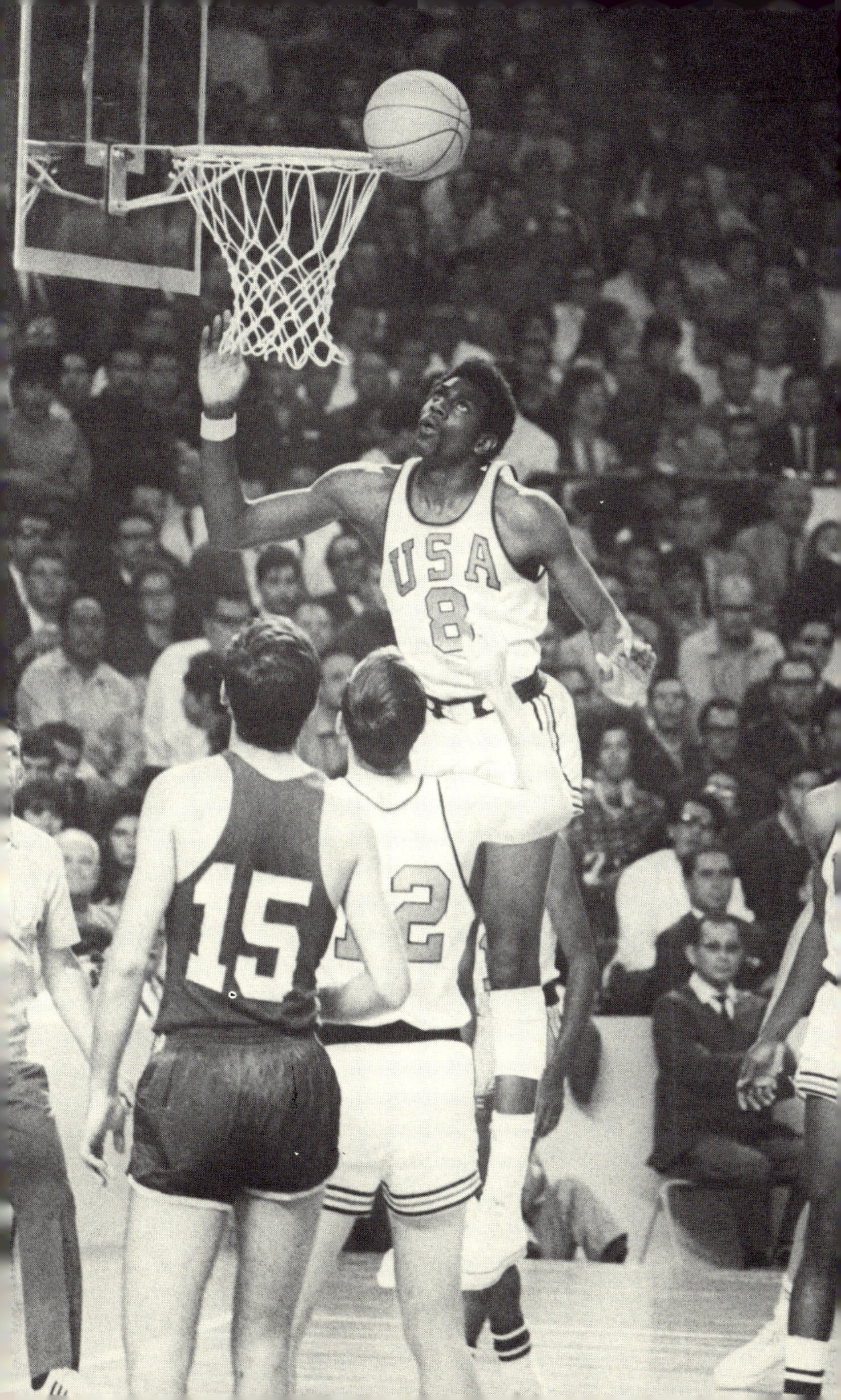
USA
8
15

After his sophomore year at Detroit, Haywood sent shudders through the basketball world by signing a $100,000-a-year contract with the Denver Rockets of the American Basketball Association. Before Haywood's signing, basketball players had to wait until their college class graduated before turning professional, but Spencer claimed that financial hardship made it impossible for him to finish school and justifiable to join the pros.

In his rookie season (1969–70) Spencer led an otherwise undistinguished Denver team to the championship playoffs and was named the league's Most Valuable Player a few days after his 21st birthday. In the fall of 1970 he made another surprising move, jumping from Denver to the Seattle SuperSonics of the rival National Basketball Association for a long-term $3-million contract.

Spencer had reached the top at an earlier age than any basketball player in history. But in his rapid climb he had made some enemies. People in Denver, Detroit, and New Mexico claimed that he had broken promises and contracts. Spencer claimed that others had broken their promises to him, and he felt justified in looking out for himself first.

He had made his way out of poverty and had succeeded in finding recognition and wealth by the time he was 21. He answered his critics by reminding them of his background: "If you're from the ghetto, it doesn't matter what you do or how you get it, only if you got it. What loyalties you got? To your family. To your [black] brothers and sisters. But to basketball? To some team? Forget it."

Mickey Mantle
COME AND TAKE ME HOME

■While some young athletes must pursue their sport over the objections of their families, many others grow up in families where sport is a way of life.

Mickey Mantle was marked as a potential baseball player almost from the day he was born. His father, Mutt Mantle, had been a good semiprofessional player who had never realized his ambition to reach the big leagues. He hoped that his son would succeed where he had failed. It would not be fair to the Mantles to say that Mickey was pushed into the game. Baseball was so much a part of his life that he seemed to assume from the beginning that it would be his career. Luckily, he had remarkable talent and eventually became a superstar with the New York Yankees.

46 ■ COME AND TAKE ME HOME

Leaving home was particularly hard for young Mickey. Unlike Rube Marquard, who left after a long argument with his father, or Spencer Haywood, who hated much that his Mississippi town stood for, Mantle was leaving a family and a community that had always encouraged and supported him. When he went off to play professional baseball he was sure to miss them.

Mickey grew up in the small town of Commerce, Oklahoma. His father was a zinc miner, and the Mantles lived frugally. Although the family could have used the extra money, Mutt Mantle would never let Mickey take after-school or summer jobs. The boy must have the chance to practice and play baseball, Mutt said. His faith in Mickey's talent soon paid off.

Mantle was discovered by a New York Yankee scout before he finished high school. The day he graduated he left to play with the Yankees' minor league team in nearby Independence, Missouri. That winter he returned home and worked part-time in the mines with his father. He also met and fell in love with Merlyn Johnson, who would one day become his wife.

The following spring, in 1950, Mickey went back to baseball. His talent was destined to move him up through the minor leagues with lightning speed. On the field he played amazingly well for one so young. But as he tells in his book

---

Mickey Mantle slams a hit in 1956—the year he was voted Most Valuable Player in the American League.

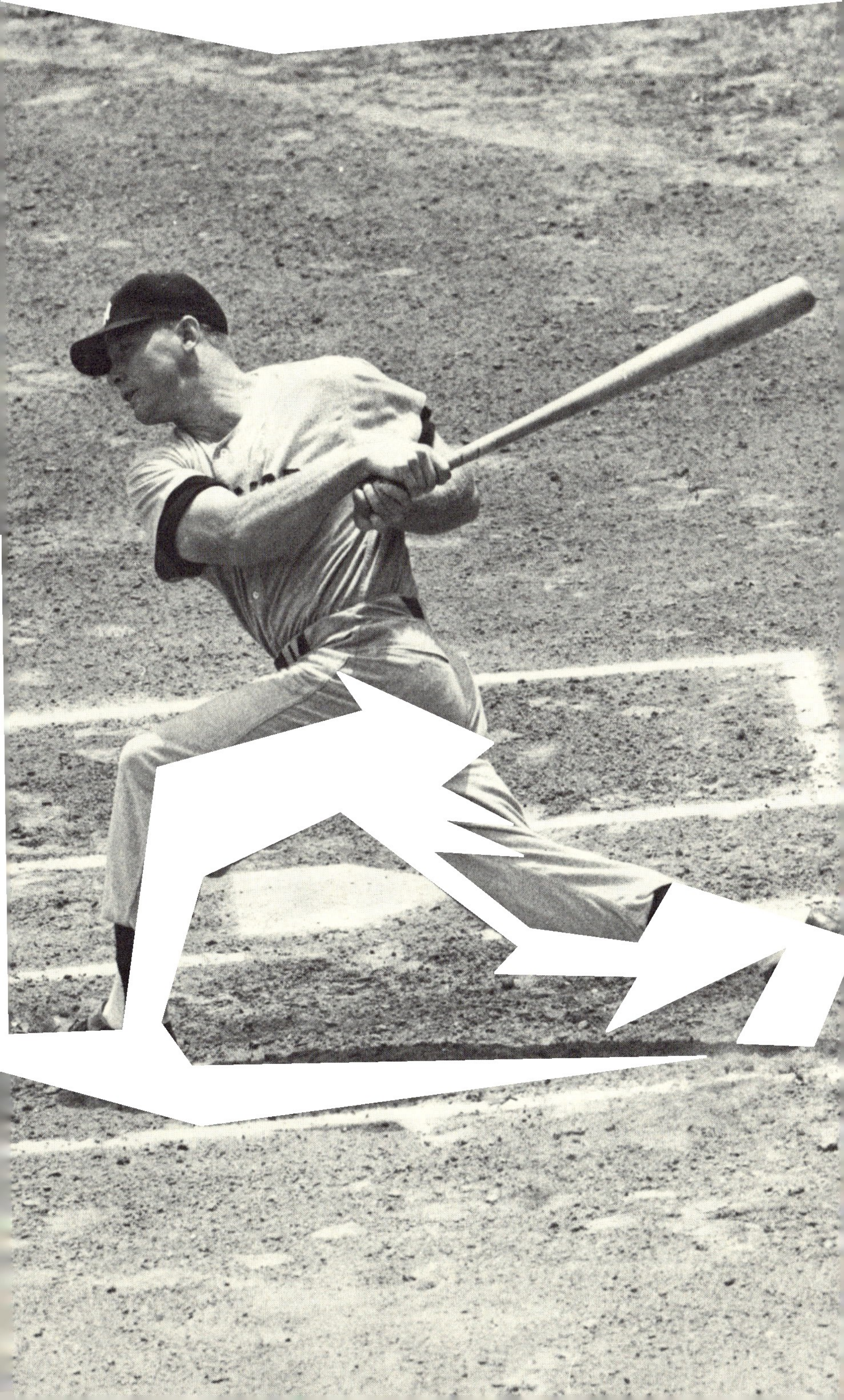

Mickey Mantle: The Education of a Baseball Player, breaking in was not as easy as it seemed.

To begin with, he was painfully shy and slow to make friends. He missed the companionship of his family and his hometown buddies. He had much to learn about the larger world that living in Commerce had not taught him. And most difficult of all, Mickey had to learn to live with the high expectations of his managers, teammates, and fans. Soon he was playing with men far older and more experienced than he, yet everyone seemed to expect miracles. When he failed to perform miracles, he began to wonder whether he was really meant to be a ballplayer after all.

It may seem strange that an athlete as talented as Mantle could have any troubles worth mentioning. But his account shows that even great advantages are no guarantee against the pains of growing up. This excerpt begins as Mickey leaves home for training camp in far-off Phoenix, Arizona, at the start of his second season of professional play.

COME AND TAKE ME HOME

My father and mother drove me down to Vinita, Oklahoma, to catch the express for Phoenix. I do believe it was one of the worst days in my life, when it should have been the gladdest. Somehow Independence had not seemed too far out of my own world. And all the time I was there, except for those first few days, I had felt at home with my teammates and especially with Harry Craft [the Independence manager who had become almost a second father to Mickey]. But now—to abandon my home heath altogether—to get so far away that you could not even telephone without spending a dollar or more—to play ball with utter strangers, older men, hardened characters—not to know anybody at all—and to have my father so far out of reach! The thought had me talking nervously on the long drive to Vinita. In the station, waiting for the train to pull in, I kept swallowing hard and drinking more water than I ever needed before.

I knew I looked pale and frightened as I turned at the steps to the train, took my suitcase in my hand, and tried to say my good-byes to my mother and father. I was just about able to speak. I got on the train, looked for a seat by the window where I could see my parents, and tried forlornly to smile as they waved up at me. The train began to roll at last and then the sobs rose up and choked me. For a whole hour I sat with my fist pressed tight to my mouth and my swimming eyes fastened unseeing on the blurred country outside as I tried to keep from weeping aloud. Tears kept welling up, in spite of me, and ran hot on my nose and cheeks. What a jerk I felt like! And how hard I tried to breathe deep and square up and look like a professional ballplayer. And how completely lost and woebegone I was!

I wished I had never left home at all and could get off at the next stop and go back to my father and mother—and to Merlyn. Sometimes I would just whisper her name out loud to take my mind off my misery.

There was nothing in Phoenix to make me feel more cheerful or more at home. The hotel where they registered me was far bigger than any I had known on the Class D circuit; the help, I thought, more distant, and the appointments more overpowering. Although most of the other players were young too, and many of them no more sophisticated than I, I made no friends and shared their company only at the ball park. There I did well. In the thin air the baseballs would go rocketing off my bat like cannon shot and I put some drives farther away than I had ever hit before. My muscles were well tuned up by the hard labor in the mine. I worked religiously at every chore the coaches set, earnestly developed a sweat at calisthenics under the desert sun, ran like a mustang, swung the bat tirelessly, and did not even sulk at my errors.

No one was really unfriendly to me, either among the rookies, or among the regulars who were acting as instructors. But the regulars had even less time for me than my fellow rookies had. I ate my meals glumly, answered when I was spoken to, holed up in my room alone in the evening, and kept asking at the desk for mail from home. It is hard for me now to convince myself that that was really me—bashful among strangers, hardly able to give my breakfast order to a waitress, and willing to spend night after night, in that warm and lively city, writing letters, reading western stories, or merely brooding in my room.

The other players all had their own friends to talk to and for all I knew may have thought me too surly to join them in their off-hour pastimes. One man I will always remember, however, as the first to show some real concern for me, and to make me feel as if I might not be wholly invisible and ignored. This was Frank Crosetti [a Yankee coach]. One day he walked up and took my ball glove out of my hand. It was my precious Playmaker model, fingers slightly scuffed, pocket soiled and well broken in.

"Where the hell did you get this?" he demanded. "You can't field a ball with that. Get yourself a decent glove."

Somehow I managed to choke out a few words to make clear that I had no money for a new glove. I had no money, as a matter of fact, even for a phone call home. Cro shrugged and walked off. But the next day he handed me a fresh new glove of the style he used himself.

The rookie school having been disbanded, with me scheduled to play with the Joplin Miners, the Yankees had no place to put me right away, so they packed me on a train for the longest trip of my life—all the way to Florida for some "conditioning" with the Kansas City club and, I suppose, a chance for some of the Yankee brass to size up their latest bargain. By the time I was finished there and had trekked back to Branson, Missouri, where the Yankees had a training camp for their lower farm clubs, all the homesickness had been scraped off me in the most painful way possible and I was beginning to feel a little like a man of the world.

Joplin was a Class C operation, with better pitching, a few more veteran players, and a higher salary limit—$3,400, pretty close to riches for playing ball all summer. But, of course, I was not earning the top salary. The best part of the move to me was not the few extra dollars but the fact that Harry Craft moved up too and right then he was the man, next to my father, whom I wanted most to be like. He taught me many things about baseball but he taught me many more things about being a man. I can't say I patterned myself after Harry, for we are two very different people. But I looked up to him, enjoyed being in his company, and found myself imitating his manner of dress and public deportment occasionally, the way boys will when they find someone they admire.

My spirits were good. I was glad to be with Harry, and I guess glad to be still more or less in my own neighborhood. Joplin, after all, was just a short hop from Baxter Springs, where I had first started to make a name for myself, so there were fans of mine all through the area to yell for me when I stepped to bat. I responded by really tying into those big fat minor league fast balls.

With the whole season to work in, and no spells of homesickness to slow me down, with a manager who never bugged me, and a club once more that was winning nearly all its games, I set records at the plate. I had 199 hits, 27 home runs, 136 runs batted in and the biggest batting average of my pro career: .383. That was one of the merriest seasons I ever lived through.

To an older player, I think, those Class C schedules could have been pretty rough, night games mostly, and long, hot bus rides, sometimes fairly primitive locker-room facilities and rock-hard playing surfaces. For a while the club had only six bats for the whole line-up. But it was a carnival to most of us, as long as those hits dropped in and those scores rolled up. Our season ended in mid-September, so the major league clubs could call up their option boys and work them out with the big team. The end of the season always meant celebrations and ceremonies, the very best of which, to me, was the day they announced the awards. I had been voted Most Valuable Player in the Western Association, and it tickled me to my bones to know my father was in the stands at Muskogee the night that announcement was made.

I expected to play some double-A or even triple-A ball along with others on the Joplin roster. Big league ball looked to me the way college looks to a high-school sophomore. But I was jumped right up to the big leagues just as soon as the season closed at Joplin—not to play in the majors, but just to travel with the Yankees and "get the feel" of belonging to the big team. By this time I had pretty well choked down the last of my homesickness and felt ready to go anywhere, in any company, without pangs. All the same, I was happy to discover that the Yankees had chosen another youngster, a hulking, good-natured, quiet type named Bill Skowron, to room with me on the trip and keep me company.

It was like a continual party—to travel with the big club, suit up in major league parks, work out in front of major league fans, and aim some of our best shots at the fences in ball parks we had only read about. Bill was a city boy, born in Chicago, and had been playing his baseball at Purdue University, so I let him take the lead in almost everything we did, figuring he knew more about how to act in a big city than I did.

The only small fret I carried on this trip was a fear my money might run out. Hotel meals were costly, so Bill and I lived largely on hamburgers and milkshakes and a lot of french fries. Not a day went by on that trip that we did not attend at least one movie. It never mattered if the show was good or bad. If it was good, we sat hypnotized to the end and then wandered out still under the spell. If it was bad, we laughed about it and repeated its worst parts to each other all the way home. But I honestly don't recall that there were so many bad ones. It seems to me that when you're that age, almost every movie is good. Some, of course, are better than others.

I got to see all the big team close up on this trip, but never felt that I knew them well. I was still too shy to approach any of them, particularly the ones like DiMaggio, who had always filled me with awe. Now, to sit right close to the great man as he stretched out his tired legs by his locker and called for a can of beer was something like having a seat near the President of the United States. I had no ambition to talk to him or even have him notice me (he did say "Hi kid!" sometimes), as long as I could gaze my fill at him when he was not looking.

Finally the team swung for St. Louis and the end of this particular idyll. I had spent pretty nearly every dime that I had held on to (after sending a good share of money home), but I did not in the least mind being broke. Just before the trip ended, Frank Scott, the road secretary, sent for me to meet him in his room. He sat there with a big checkbook before him and asked me briskly, "Now what have your expenses been on this trip? If you'll let me have the totals of your meal checks and so on, I'll give you your expense check."

I was honestly astounded, almost unable to speak. Expenses! When I spoke, it was just above a whisper. "Is the club going to *pay* me for the *meals* I ate?"

Frank laughed out loud. I must have been a picture of the country boy on his first trip away from home.

"Well, Mr. Weiss [the Yankee general manager] said I should be good to you," he said. "And we certainly expected to pay for your meals."

My God! All those hamburgers and french fries! Or rather, all those steaks that Bill and I passed up! Frank added up the days, multiplied them by some incredible sum of money—$10 or so, twice as much as I would have spent—and handed me a check. I had actually made a profit on the deal and I went home to Commerce so happy I could have made the whole distance in a series of jumps. So this is what it was like to be a Yankee!

The next spring I went to Phoenix once more, feeling far more at ease this time, strong from an active winter, and ready to enjoy sending those baseballs streaking through that unresisting air. There was a collection of rookies there and one or two were far less at home than I was, so my own lonesomeness was somewhat reduced.

The men on the field, chiefly Bobby Brown and Jerry Coleman, who played on either side of me when I tried to be a shortstop, were endlessly helpful and patient. But after I had worked out in the infield one day, Casey [Stengel, the Yankee manager] came over to me and said mildly, "Ever think of playing the outfield?" Then, as now, I was ready to play anywhere my manager asked me to and I was glad to have Tommy Henrich take me over to make me into an outfielder.

Gradually I became more at home with the club, although I was a long way from feeling like a Yankee. But this time I knew I was learning major league ball and I ate up my lessons and put my whole heart in my practice.

There were many things about the game that I needed no coaching on. On the bases, Casey turned me loose, because he saw that I knew how to get a start on a pitcher and he had no fear that I would miss a chance. I didn't have to be taught how to catch a ball and while I more than once threw the ball to the wrong base after a catch, Casey corrected me in a kindly way and told me what was right and why. There must have been many young players as dumb as I was and probably a few even dumber, but I did all the same manage to pull some rocks that nobody else could match.

In one of our early exhibitions I played center field with Gene Woodling beside me in right. It was the first big league competition for me, for we were playing Cleveland and we were out to win. Early in the game I got my very first big league chance. Ray Boone hit a line drive straight at me. It was easy to line up and I moved in a few steps to take it chest high. The sun was bright and, in order to look professional in every way, I flipped my sunglasses down with a practiced finger. As soon as I did, the day went black! I was not looking into the sun and the ball disappeared completely. Before I could react to this phenomenon, the ball hit me square on the head, just above my nose, and bounced off as if it had struck a rock. I staggered for a second, pulled the glasses back, and looked foggily for the ball. It had bounded high, but not far, and Gene Woodling, ranging close, fielded it quickly and threw it in. Then he came back to me, and I tried to look suitably pained, apologetic, and bewildered. Actually, I did not have to try too hard, for the wallop had left me woozy and had raised a lump. And I was fiercely embarrassed. But Gene was not concerned with the state of my health or my soul.

"You break the glasses?" he demanded. I reached up numbly to examine them. "They're okay," I said. I wondered if I should tell him that *I* was not, but he just turned and trotted back to his position. I suppose he figured any kid dumb enough to blind himself that way must have a head hard enough to withstand a line drive.

But I did my share of good things too, mostly at the plate, and the approval of my new teammates came quickly and made my life easier. We worked our way gradually to New York, where we were to "open" with exhibition games against the Dodgers, then shove off to Washington to open the regular season in front of the President. Before the first game at the Stadium I came down early to the park—it is just a few blocks from the hotel where I stayed—and walked out on the grass to look up at the sweep of empty stands. Gee, it was big! There was not another place like it in the country just then. I tried to imagine it jammed with people, and me there at the plate driving a baseball out into those distant, dark seats. Well, that, I told myself, was still a year or two away.

The two or three other rookies who had been held over

Mickey Mantle (right) gets advice from Yankee manager Casey Stengel during his rookie season in 1951.

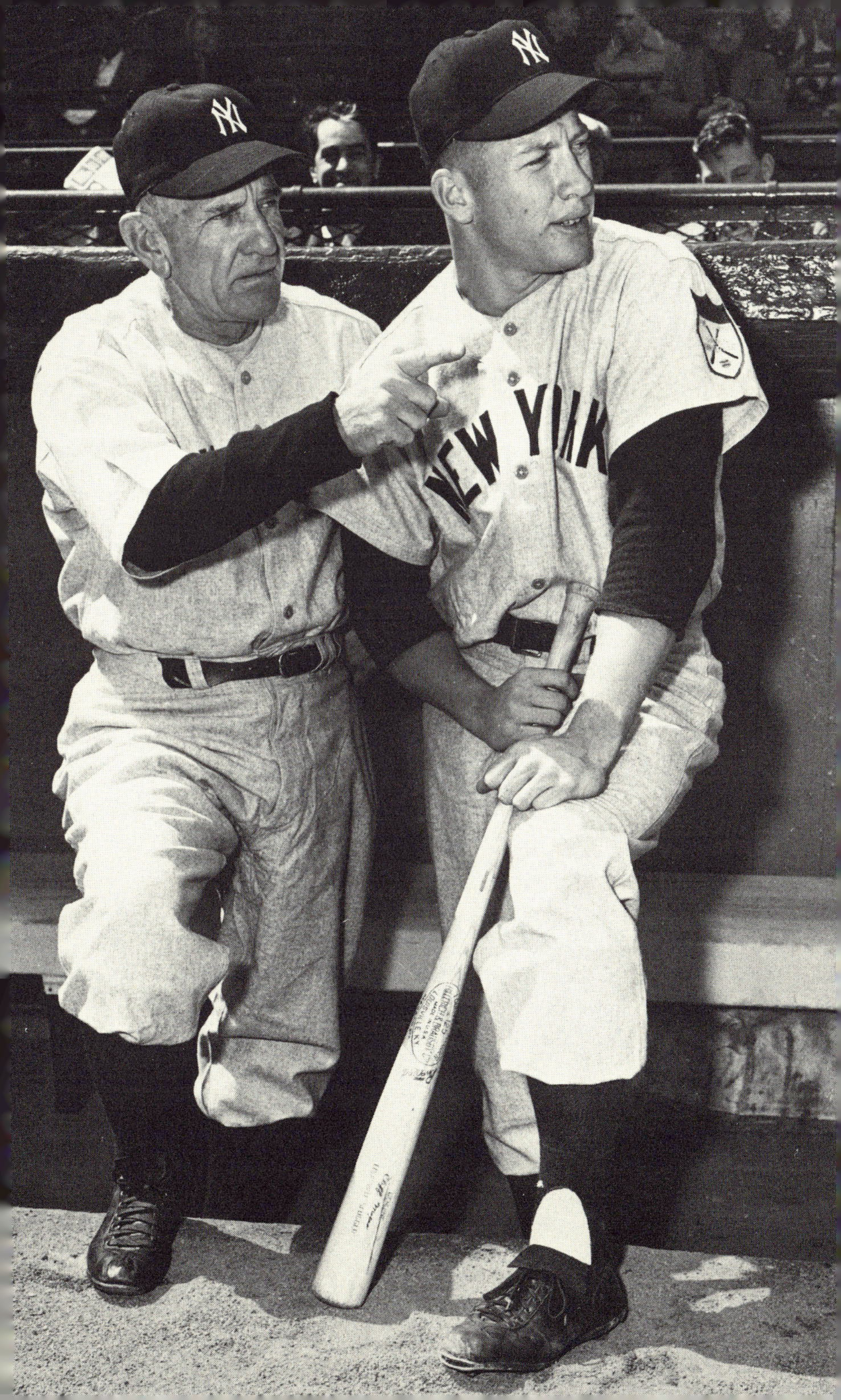
NEW YORK

with the big team were slated to go to Binghamton now that the big league season was about to open. But the Yankees had another Class A club in Beaumont, Texas, and I knew that Harry Craft had been sent there. I was trying to get up nerve enough to tell Casey I would like to go to Beaumont too. But it was not until we were on the train to Washington that I found courage enough to ask Casey about this. I made a point of explaining that I wanted to be where Harry Craft was going to be. Casey squinted hard at me.

"How'd you like to stay with the Yankees?" he said.

The Yankees! How could that be? Jump from Class C to the *Yankees?* When I got my breath back, I made it plain to Casey that a miracle like that, if it could be worked, would put about an inch of frosting on my cake.

"All right," said Casey. "You come back here with me and meet Mr. Weiss. You let me do the talking. I'm going to see if I can get you a little more than the minimum."

The minimum then was $5,000 and that was more money than my father made. To get more than that meant that I could practically take over support of the family, or at least make things a whole lot easier for them . . . Or get married . . . Or . . . I could not begin to think of all the things I might be able to do with so much money in my pocket. In a sort of pink haze I trailed after Casey to the drawing room where George Weiss and Dan Topping sat.

The deal was made and I could feel myself beginning to grin all over. My first impulse when we got out of the drawing room was to run and telephone my father. But even if there had been a telephone on that train, I'd have not known how to use it or dared to try. So I sat down and savored my good luck all by myself in the Pullman chair. Before I could even write my father about it, he had learned through the newspapers that I had signed a Yankee contract.

My big league career was all over (I thought) in a matter of weeks. I was doing reasonably well at the plate and had managed to handle nearly everything that came my way in the outfield, with only one or two real dumb mistakes. Then the club went to Boston and a long, lean right-hander named Masterson struck me out five times. Each time I faced him I seemed to get worse. I would get one high, inside fast ball after another, the kind any strong batter ought to be able to drive out of the park, and I would miss the ball each time by what seemed to me at least twelve inches. I was always going for the distance anyway, unless I was bunting, so I really stirred that Boston air, until it must have ruffled the feathers of the harbor gulls. I had not been so handcuffed, or so humiliated, since I started taking money for playing ball. I knew a lot of curse words by that time and I applied them all, out loud, to myself, as I returned each time to the bench and, once under cover, I took a kick at the water cooler. If someone had showed me a baseball right then, I believe I'd have grabbed up my bat and knocked it right out of his hand, and probably have torn his hand off with it.

In the locker room I never spoke to anyone anyway, because I was simply too bashful to start a conversation. So mostly I brooded in silence on what Masterson had done to me. Then it came to me that another lanky pitcher in my past had made a public idiot of me several times, and I had eventually cured him by dragging bunts. I made up my mind that next time I would do exactly the same. I was as fast as anyone I had met in the majors and I knew that if I could not hit a pitcher, I could surely outrun him.

This thought provided me comfort enough so that my spirits had lifted by the time we reached Detroit. In *this* game, I promised myself, I would get on base if I had to break an ankle trying.

Before the game began, Casey called me to his cubbyhole, to give me some advice, I imagined, about dealing with high, inside pitches. I was all ready to explain what I would do next time. But next time, I suddenly learned, was not coming. In a perfectly gentle way, but with complete bluntness, Casey told me I was being sent to Kansas City. I don't believe he quite realized what he was doing to me. He gave me the usual assurances that I would be back up, but I took this for no more than a crude effort to take the curse off the sentence he had just passed.

I went blindly and wordlessly back to the hotel and started at once for Minneapolis, where the Kansas City club was playing. Casey probably assumed that, as I had been ready to go to Beaumont, in double-A ball, it would be no serious jolt to find myself in Kansas City, which was triple-A then. But he might as well have told me he was shipping me back to Independence. I had been a Yankee, and now I was nothing. I was always one of those guys who took all bad luck doubly hard, who saw disaster when there was just everyday trouble, and who took every slump as if it were a downhill slide to oblivion. The trip to Minneapolis was mercifully short, but I remember none of it. I was too choked up to tell anyone good-bye and too blind with misery to take any note of passing scenery.

With Kansas City I had a momentary resurgence of hope when I told myself that I would make a quick comeback by dragging a bunt safely, and showing Casey and everybody else that I *could* get on base any time I wanted. So in my very first time at bat, against a right-hander, I picked out a good pitch, ran to meet it and put it neatly down where the pitcher could not reach it. I made first base with a yard to spare and stood there trying to look properly blasé, but feeling almost good enough to smile again. When the inning was over, I trotted modestly in to the bench to pick up my glove, and manager George Selkirk gave me a sour look that startled me.

"They didn't send you down here to bunt!" he growled. "They sent you down here to hit."

That finished me. I felt like the little boy who brought

home a mud pie for a present and got himself a licking. As I went out to my position, I could feel the tears of self-pity stinging my eyes. What did a guy have to do? I asked myself.

What I did was go to bat twenty-two times in a row without a hit. Whatever I had had, I told myself, I had lost it now and my baseball career was over. It had all been too good too soon anyway, and I had no more heart for the big leagues or even for triple-A. I would go back home, take my job in the mines, play ball for money in the summer, and save up to marry Merlyn. I knew my father would sympathize with me, for he had had his own disappointments in baseball. I really longed to have him beside me, to put his arm over my shoulder and tell me that it was all right, that I had tried and failed, and that everybody was looking forward to having me home again. For a time I had been ashamed to write him of my disgrace, but now I asked him to come meet me in Kansas City and take me home. Home. That word never sounded so full of comfort before.

When my father met me in Kansas City, I could not speak for crying. My throat was squeezed tight and tears ran down my cheeks. But my father's eyes were ablaze. He started in on me without preliminaries:

"If that's the way you're going to take this," he said, "you don't belong in baseball anyway. If you have no more guts than that, just forget about the game completely. Come back and work in the mines, like me."

His tone, as much as his words, went right down through me and froze my toes. There was not a trace of sympathy in his eye. I had been looking for a comforting pat on the back and I had not even gotten a handshake. Get back on the field and play ball, he told me, if you've got the guts for it, and if not, then make up your mind right now you're through with the game for good.

I wanted to tell him that I *had* tried, that I had been up at bat twenty-three times with only a bunt single to show for it. But I knew better than to argue with my father when he was in this mood. I just had to bite back my shock and surprise and tell him I wanted to stay and try to do what he wanted me to do.

I did too. With his words still searing the underside of my soul, I went to bat that night and hit two home runs and I felt so damn good about it I nearly broke into tears anyway. And that night I got the handshake and the pat on the back that I had longed for. And I began to suspect that I had grown into a man.

That, I think, was the greatest thing my father ever did for me. All the encouragement he had given me when I was small, all the sacrifices he had made so I could play ball when other boys were working in the mines, all the painstaking instruction he had provided—all these would have been thrown away if he had not been there that night to put the iron into my spine when it was needed most.

I played in about 35 more games for Kansas City that

year and had 121 more at bats. In that time I got 57 more hits, including 9 home runs, 3 triples, and 9 doubles. Altogether I knocked in 50 runs and ran my batting average up to .360 before Stengel decided I had perhaps learned a little about my strike zone and sent for me to come back to the big team.

This time I knew I was going to stay.

■That fall Mickey appeared in the World Series with the Yankees. His father and mother came all the way from Oklahoma to watch him play. In the second game Mickey tripped on a drainpipe in the outfield at Yankee Stadium and seriously injured his knee. Just outside the hospital where Mickey was being taken, Mutt Mantle collapsed. Father and son watched the rest of the Series side by side in hospital beds.

Mickey recovered from his knee injury, but his father was discovered to have Hodgkin's disease, a form of cancer. He lingered through the winter, but the next spring, before Mickey began his second season with the Yankees, Mutt Mantle died. Mickey played 17 more seasons for the Yankees, becoming one of the great stars of the 1950s and 1960s. Mutt Mantle didn't live to see his son's greatest triumphs, but he had done his work well—Mickey had grown up and could face the world by himself.

Anthony Quinn
WHY DIDN'T YOU THROW THAT RIGHT?

■For every big winner in sport, there are hundreds of losers. Of the thousands of boys who want to play baseball or football, few ever get to play in the minor leagues or in college, and fewer than one in a thousand plays even a single game in the majors. Sport is ruthlessly selective, and only a handful of athletes are good enough and devoted enough to reach big-time competition.

In the early 1930s Anthony Quinn was a poor boy of Irish and Mexican parentage who lived in a run-down section of Los Angeles. At 15, he had lost interest in school, yet he wasn't old enough to get a full-time job. Then he discovered his sport—boxing.

Boxing has made many poor boys rich and famous, but

Tony Quinn wasn't one of them. He had many of the qualities of a good fighter, but one was lacking. His sports career ended almost before it began. Years later he did become rich and famous—as an Academy-Award-winning film star. When he wrote *The Original Sin*, an account of his life, his boxing days were just a small episode in his boyhood.

Those who drop out of athletic competition are seldom moved to write about their failures. If Anthony Quinn had not become famous in another pursuit, we probably would not have had this story to represent the thousands for whom sport is a passing phase, not a lifetime career.

WHY DIDN'T YOU THROW THAT RIGHT?

One day I ran into a kid named Buddy, whom I hadn't seen for some time. He was wearing a flashy new suit and two-toned shoes. I asked him if he'd pulled a job. He told me he was making twenty-five dollars a night.

"Doing what?" I gasped, hoping to get a hot tip.

"Boxing," he said, throwing a fast jab that missed me by a whisker.

Of course, I thought to myself, what an idiot I'd been. Dempsey and Gene Tunney had become millionaires from

Anthony Quinn as he looked in his mid-twenties.

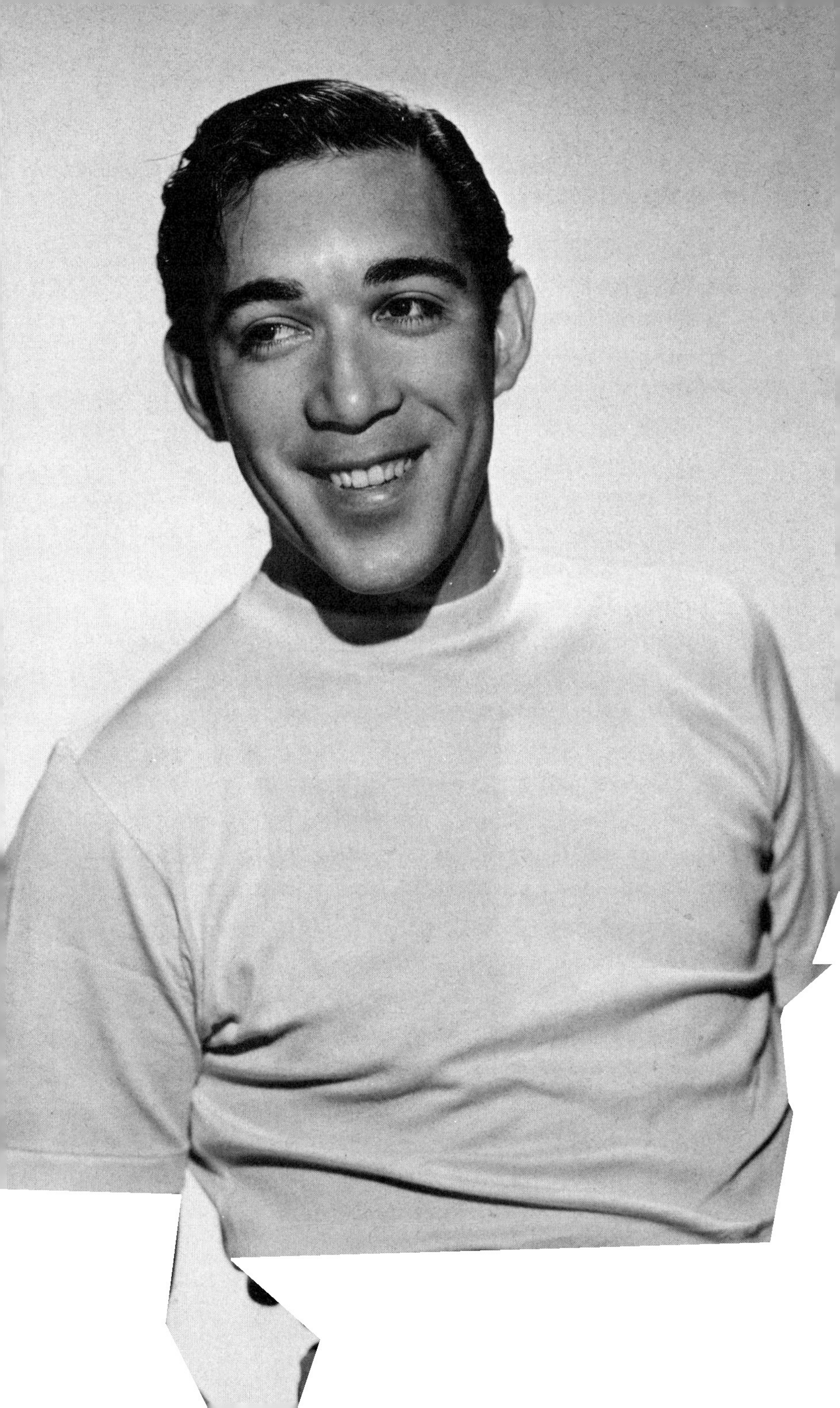

one fight. I swiftly saw myself as the champion of the world, with a deadly right cross. Buddy gave me an address of a man who booked smokers [boxing matches held in private clubs].

Next day, I went to Spring Street and waited in a long line of aspiring pugilists to be interviewed by a big heavy-set man sitting behind a desk. The walls were covered with idols of mine—Newsboy Brown, Mushy Callahan, Bert Colima, Dynamite Jackson, Gentleman Gen del Monte, Tunney, Dempsey. I couldn't wait till my picture would grace the wall. I knew exactly the kind of pose I'd assume: my chin tucked into my left shoulder and my dynamic right cocked for the knockout blow. I'd wear a sneering smile, but my eyes would be cold and hard.

The man asked me what weight I fought under. I said "Welterweight." He gave me a slip of paper. "Give this to the man out front." I was booked to fight in Gardena in a four rounder. The winner was to get five dollars, the loser three.

Buddy took me under his wing. I did two miles of roadwork at the crack of dawn around Echo Park Lake. He taught me how to bob and weave. I was tall for my age, but weighed only a hundred and forty-five pounds. As the great night approached, I began to feel I could use a hell of a lot more time preparing. Buddy kept assuring me he'd be in my corner when I made my debut, so I felt better. He and I rode the red streetcar to Gardena, where the businessmen were still at dinner. They were all having a hell of a time. As I crossed the hall toward the dressing rooms I heard some man say, "Kid, I'm betting on you." I nodded, reassuring him he could rest easy, his money was riding on the future champion of the world. Buddy had brought his fighting togs for me to use. Now that it was about to happen I began to feel fear as I had never known it in my life. Not so much of being hurt as of being ridiculous in front of all those men. Several other guys came into the dressing room and changed. Very little was said. I figured they were all going through the same qualms I was having.

Buddy told me to warm up. He held his hands up for me to hit. My own were heavily bandaged. Then I put on the gloves. They were much heavier than I had anticipated. I was to go on in the third bout.

Someone came into the room and told me the first fight had ended in a knockout, and the second wasn't going to last long. We went to the door to see how the fight was coming along. A tall dark stringy kid was reeling under the punishment a husky blond boy was dealing out. Some men were yelling: "Kill the greezer." "In the belly, hit the Mexican in the belly." The tall kid dropped stiff as a board from a looping right. He didn't stir as the referee counted him out. His handlers rushed into the ring and carried him through the aisles to a dressing room.

Buddy pushed me toward the ring. Suddenly, I was under the glare of the overhead lights. Buddy was rubbing my back as the referee called the other kid and me to the center of the ring for instructions. I barely heard what was said. I kept looking at the boy I was going to fight. He never looked at me. He kept staring at the floor. It was only when the bell rang for the fight to begin that I saw the fear in his eyes.

Though I had run miles training for the fight, I never knew how long twelve minutes of fighting can be. By the end of the fourth round I could barely lift my hands. I can't say it was the most exciting fight in the annals of fisticuffs, but we both earned our money. Buddy had done a good job of teaching me how to bob and weave and throw a jab. I was awarded the decision.

It was a happy ride back home that night on the streetcar. We had been fed well by some men who had bet on me. So I was on my way to fame and fortune. I could see myself as a contender for the title, with a big roadster full of blonds.

After that first night I fought quite regularly. Along about the eighth or ninth fight, I was booked to meet a red-headed kid who was making a name for himself. He was chunky, with arms like hams. When we met in the center of the ring I could see hate in his eyes. All the other guys had tried to scare me by looking mean and tough, but I somehow knew it was all an act. This guy really made me feel he hated me, that he would have killed me with no compunction. When the bell rang I knew I was in for a bad night. Buddy had insisted I run backward a half a mile every morning, an exercise I put to good use that night.

During the first round, the red-headed kid threw a left hook at my kidney and I blocked the punch with my right, hurting it. For the rest of the round I wasn't able to lift it. I fought to survive. Buddy used to tell me I had style, that I looked good in the ring. That particular night I fought very well, despite a bruised right, and beat the boy. After the fight a man came in to the little dressing room and said that he'd been watching me. He thought I could be great. "How old are you?" I was sixteen at the time, but I lied and said I was eighteen, the minimum legal age for fighting at smokers.

He said, "Well, if you let me train you, I promise to make you a champion." I said that was fine. "How many smokers have you fought?" I lied. I told him a dozen. "All right, kid, from now on we don't fight any smokers; we don't do any of this. Do you need money?" I nodded.

"All right, I'm going to give you ten dollars a week. You don't have to fight yet, but you have to train. You fight when I tell you to fight." I said, "Fine, all right. But excuse me, who are you?"

"I'm Jim Foster."

Well, it was like saying to me, "I'm the President of the United States," because he was well known at that time as a star manager. When he said he wanted to handle me, it was almost like a guarantee that I would become a champion.

I went home and told all the kids. Buddy was impressed, though he was a much better fighter than I was. He said, "All right, I'll train with you." We used to get up in the morning, put on heavy sweaters, sweat clothes, and go out and run two or three miles around Echo Park. Then we would shadowbox. When I came home, I'd have a big breakfast and a nap. I was living like a real boxer. In the afternoon after school, which I attended periodically, I would meet Buddy at a Main Street gym, where I saw the big stars, Sandy Casanova, Newsboy Brown, Mushy Callahan and others.

I seldom saw Mr. Foster. He had made arrangements for me to get into the gym, and was paying the fees. And people there were very impressed. I could hear them whisper, "That's one of Foster's boys."

He appointed a trainer who supervised me, correcting my faults. Among others, I had developed a very strong left hand at the expense of my right.

Eventually, Jim sent me out to fight. In those days they had boxing rings in every little town—Anaheim, Long Beach, Downey, Watts, all along the periphery of Los Angeles. Usually, managers kept thirty per cent of whatever you made, but I was making so little that Jim would give me all my money. I was getting anywhere from twenty to thirty dollars a fight.

There are different categories on boxing cards: the semi-windup, the preliminaries, and the headliners. I was usually third or fourth on the list, already heading for some kind of stardom. I won all my fights.

Jim selected the fighters I was to meet, boys he thought

wouldn't be too tough on me, and when I'd had about thirteen or fourteen fights he said he was going to get me a semi-windup. That's like saying to an actor, "I'm going to give you the second lead in a picture." The only drawback was that the fight was in Watts, and there were certain neighborhoods that we hated to go to because the kids were very tough. Watts had the toughest.

I went out there and I fought, and I was very lucky; I beat the boy and had no trouble. I had made good on my first semi-windup, and the trainer congratulated me. I made a lot of money that day, fifty dollars. So I became a big guy in the neighborhood, and, of course, all my friends were proud of me.

Then I had another preliminary fight, this one in Downey, and I won that. And finally the trainer said, "Well, Tony. Kid, I think you're ready. We're going to get you a good boy to fight, then we'll talk about maybe going some place outside of Los Angeles, San Francisco or maybe San Diego, and you can really start making a reputation for yourself."

They got me a fight in Long Beach. It was a semi-windup against a black boy. The stadium was full. As I was waiting in the dressing room, Buddy was there rubbing my shoulders, and all my pals showed up, Willy and Sidney and everybody, and it was like I was making the big time, like I was suddenly appearing on Broadway. Of course, I was nervous as hell. You were always nervous before a fight.

Finally, somebody called, "All right, you're on, kid!" and

I put on the robe my grandmother had made for me—made specifically to Bud's specifications. My grandmother wasn't very much for my boxing, but I was bringing money into the house and she never saw me getting hurt, so I had been able to convince her that it was all right. I had been very lucky up until then. I had never been scratched or marked very much. Most of the boys of my age had broken noses or teeth, or cauliflower ears. But I had been lucky. Of course, at the smokers we'd fought with bigger gloves, not with eight-ounce gloves as you did in the semi-windups.

So I was walking down the aisle and suddenly people started calling my name. Most kids at that time chose some kind of fighting name. I didn't. I always liked the name Tony Quinn. It meant something to me and I never wanted to change it.

As I climbed into the ring my friends started applauding and yelling and the crowd decided it liked me. When the black boy I was to fight walked up the aisle, they started booing. Sometimes audiences will do that in a fight and it is supposed to be good-natured fun, but I always thought there was something sad about it. I felt sorry for the boy. As he climbed into the ring, I heard somebody say, "Hey, Smoky, this kid's going to kill you." Smoky meant Negro, and not in a complimentary way. I didn't like it. My friend Buddy was black, too, and there in the ring with me as my second; he was the guy that would hand me the water to gargle between rounds. He was rubbing a towel on me and I was embarrassed that Buddy had heard it.

The referee called us together to give us instructions. You hear the same goddamned instructions every time you fight; it's a silly, ridiculous ritual: "All right, boys, I want a good fight—keep it clean. When I touch you on the elbow, that means break. Don't hit in the clinches . . . et cetera." Nobody is listening. Everybody is worrying about his own problems. You're sizing up the other boy and you try to avoid his eyes. But I couldn't avoid this boy's eyes; and as I looked up he was gazing at me, as if to say, "What's going to happen?" There was something in the boy's eyes that I liked.

We went back to our corners and Buddy put in my mouthpiece. It was really a used mouthpiece of his. The way he put it in my mouth, the way he looked at me, I felt like saying, "Gee, how can I fight one of your people, Buddy?" God only knows what he was thinking.

Suddenly the bell rang and the boy came right at me. By that time, I had learned to be kind of a fancy dancer and I sidestepped, shot a left at him that connected, feinted a right cross, and hit him a left in the stomach. The boy was rather surprised at my speed. He hit me a couple of times and got me over in a corner, but I had learned a lot of tricks from Buddy. I took the boy's elbow and pushed him away and hit him with a right cross. I had good concentration. The fight now was really fun. I had fought boys who weren't that good, but this boy was classy, so I had to show my best.

78 ■ WHY DIDN'T YOU THROW THAT RIGHT?

The first round went well. In the second I could do almost anything I wanted and I heard people saying, "Knock him out! Knock him out!" I feinted with the right, the boy would drop his hand, and I'd throw in the hook; but I could only fight well with my left hand. I won the second round too. Buddy said to me, "Come on, step up the fight!" I said, "What's the difference, Buddy? I can beat him. It's a six-round fight, why knock him out?" He said, "You're fighting, that's why."

In the fourth round, I felt so comfortable that I thought I could really beat the boy any time I wanted. I got a little careless. Suddenly he caught me with a right, and I had never felt a punch as strong. The fact that I could be hit, that I could be stunned, shocked me. I found myself against the ropes. The stadium was going around and all I saw was this form come up. I crouched down and covered my head. He hit me with a left hook and miraculously everything cleared. He could probably have knocked me out but the fact that he hit me on the other side of the head kind of stabilized me. I was back in focus, able to finish the round. I was never so happy to hear the bell in my life, because I was really in trouble.

When I went back to the corner, Buddy was furious because I hadn't followed up my advantage in the beginning

---

Anthony Quinn in 1964 as Zorba the Greek, one of his most memorable film roles.

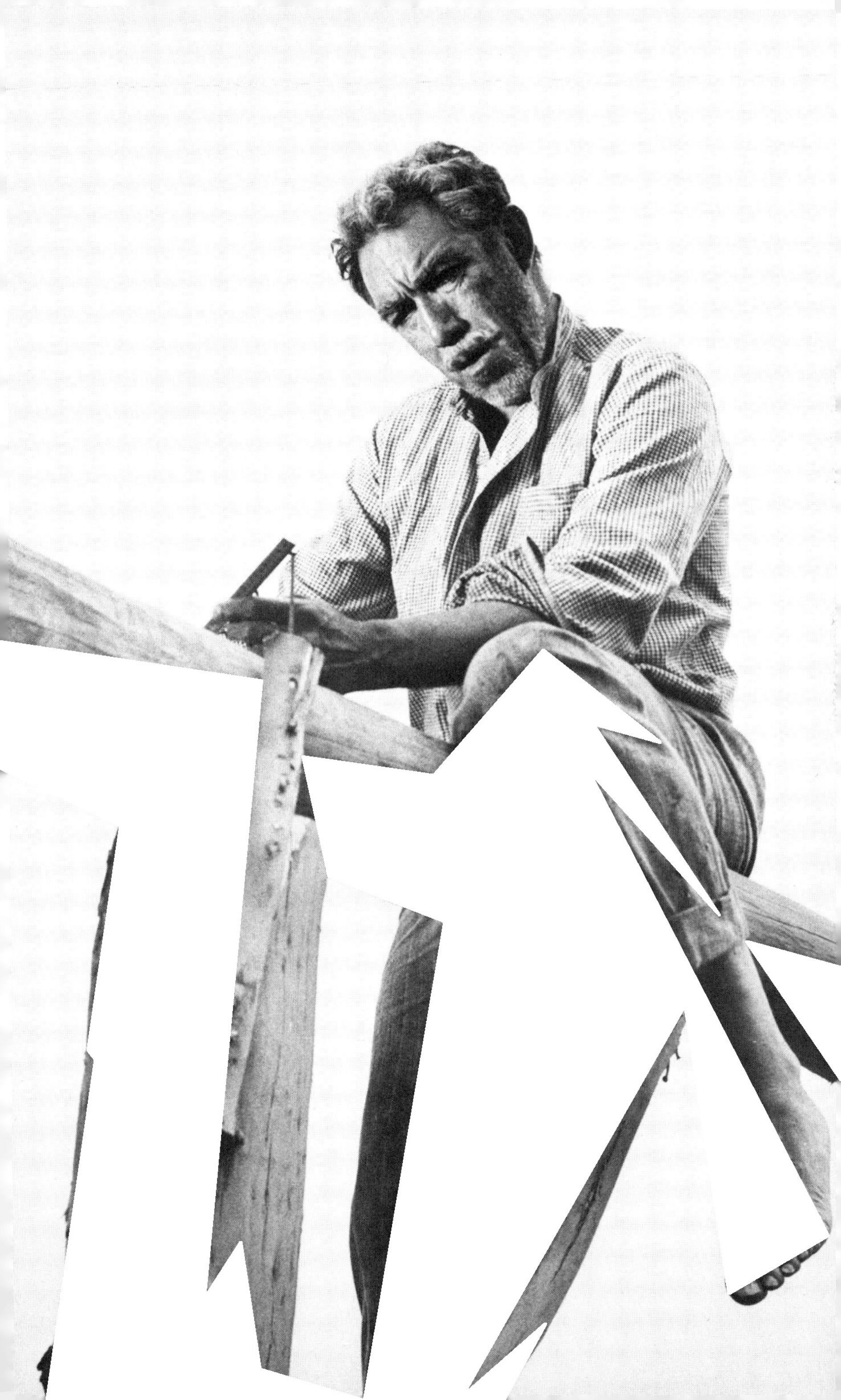

of the round and had let the boy catch me. The fifth round was coming up. Buddy said, "All right, go out and get him." I must admit I felt that if I didn't get the boy now he was going to get me. Because I'd won the first four rounds, I still had a slight advantage. I was wary now, more careful of the boy's right hand. The crowd was urging me to come back, but I was still in a partial daze from his fight.

Almost a minute into the fifth round, I feinted with a right and caught the boy with a hard left. His guard went down and I kept hitting him with my left. I threw a right at his stomach, he bent down, I hit him again with a left hook, and he began to reel. I heard these people near the apron of the ring chant, "Come on, kill the nigger!"

I remembered a year before when I had had a fight at school and I hadn't been able to hit the boy because they had been calling him a Jew. Here they were begging me to "kill the nigger." I didn't follow up my advantage. The boy straightened up and started moving away. I just kept jabbing him. I could hear Buddy calling to me, saying, "Throw the right!" The boy's guard was down and I saw his jaw unprotected. I knew that if I threw the right I could nail him, but I felt blocked. I couldn't throw my right. I kept jabbing. The bell rang, we went back to our corners, and again Buddy bawled me out.

I couldn't say to him that I couldn't hit the boy because of what the crowd was yelling. I told him not to worry, that I was winning by a big margin.

The bell for the sixth round came up. The crowd had less interest in me because I hadn't thrown a right hand in the round before. They seemed to be with the black boy now. I heard somebody yell, "Come on, hit the Mexican, he's yellow!" I turned for a second to see who had been talking when a hammer blow hit me on the right side of my jaw. It felt like my jaw had cracked; everything started reeling. I had become a piece of wood. I couldn't move my jaw and I couldn't stand up and I couldn't fall down. I felt a hard blow on my stomach. I tried to get against the ropes, but my legs were paralyzed. Next thing I knew, I was on the canvas, surprised as hell. I heard the referee count. At the count of seven I tried to get up. I got up on one knee . . . at nine, I started to get off my knee . . . and I collapsed. I just couldn't make it. That was the first time I was ever knocked out in the ring.

Buddy came and picked me up. He sat me in the corner, washed my face with cold water, sprinkled some water over my head, and I came to. I had no more than a slight headache. I wasn't too hurt at having lost. I realized that I had paid for one moment of carelessness, but I didn't feel I had put on a bad fight.

When I got back to the dressing room, which we shared with all the other fighters, Jim Foster walked in. I looked up sheepishly as if to say, "Well, it's no disgrace, the best fighters in the world get knocked out." But he was furious at me.

"Why didn't you throw that right in the fifth round?"

"Well, I didn't have a chance."

"The boy was wide open. You had him reeling. Why didn't you throw a right?"

"I thought he was just faking and trying to suck me in. Look, get me another fight with him and I promise you I'll beat him."

"Not only will I not get you another fight with him, but if I ever see you in the ring again, I, myself, will climb up and beat the hell out of you."

I was surprised by the tone in his voice. He sounded like an angry father reprimanding a son he loves very much.

"I never want to see you in the ring again. You're not a killer, and you don't belong in this game unless you're a killer."

On the way home I said to Buddy, who had witnessed the scene with Foster, "Gee, Bud, what do you think?"

And Bud said, "I think Jim's right. I don't think you should fight."

I knew he was right. I had no killer instinct, I would never make a great fighter.

Although I liked the glamorous part of boxing, the performance part of it, I didn't like the competitiveness. I liked the drama, those bright lights, the kind of strangely festive atmosphere in the audience, and the comradeship with the guys. I hated the dressing room with its odors of rubbing alcohol, iodine, wet leather, cheap soap and dirty, stained towels. I hated the tawdriness behind the scenes, all those sweating bodies, the frantic efforts to achieve something with your fists.

That night my grandmother said she was happy about what had happened. She thought it was for the best, and she had been praying for some months that I would stop. I think we both knew, deep down, that it was just a stopgap to get some money.

A few days later, I ran into Baby Ariesmendi, one of the world's greatest fighters. He had started fighting just to strengthen his legs, because he'd been afflicted with polio, and ended up becoming the champion of the world in his class.

The week before, I had seen him in a fight with one of the top boxers of his era, Lew Ambers. In the seventh round, Ambers had caught Baby against the ropes.

I said to him, "Baby, I saw that fight between you and Lew Ambers, and in the seventh round he hit you hard. Did he hurt you?"

It was a long time before he answered. "Tony, everybody hurts you."

Smith

Dave Meggyesy
I WAS PLAYING FOR SURVIVAL

■Some athletes, like Anthony Quinn, leave competition because they discover something lacking in themselves. Others, like Dave Meggyesy, find something lacking in their sport.

In 1969 Meggyesy was a 28-year-old linebacker for the St. Louis Cardinals in the National Football League. A rough and aggressive player, he had been a star since high school. But over several years he had also developed other interests, particularly politics. In 1968 and 1969 he became involved in the protest movement to end the war in Vietnam. He soon

Dave Meggyesy at 28, soon after he announced his retirement from football.

discovered that his team's owners, his coaches, and many teammates did not look kindly on his activities. In fact, coaches sent him into games less often, presumably because of his antiwar statements and activities.

At the same time, Meggyesy was beginning to have his doubts about football itself, and after the 1969 season he quit. In spite of their disapproval of his politics, the Cardinals offered him $35,000 a year and a promise that he would play regularly if he would return. But Meggyesy refused the offer. "They couldn't offer me anything that would get me back into a football uniform and out onto the field," he wrote later.

After his retirement, Meggyesy wrote *Out of Their League,* a book about his life in football. Many football coaches and players like to say that the game teaches the high ideals of teamwork, sacrifice, and hard, clean competition. But for Meggyesy and others like him, the sport miserably failed to live up to its claims.

Meggyesy's disillusionment colors his account of his high school football experiences in the 1950s. He had been an intense, gung-ho player. But looking back, he concludes that the values he had to accept to be a top football player were false and harmful. He sees a kind of inhumanity in the game itself, and suggests that he escaped the brutality of his home only to discover more brutality in football.

Like some of the others in this book, Meggyesy used sports as a way out of poverty and unhappiness. Unlike the others, he felt in the end that he was a victim rather than a victor.

I WAS PLAYING FOR SURVIVAL

Looking back now, I realize many of the conditions that got me into a pro uniform and onto the football field were there from the very beginning.

I was born in Cleveland on November 1, 1941. My father had come to America from Hungary when he was nine years old and never got over the trauma of being an emigrant. He spent his youth farming strawberries in Louisiana and then came up to the big city to work as a tool and die maker. But by the time our family started to grow, he decided that urban life was becoming too dangerous. He had been doing some union organizing and things hadn't worked out very well. So when I was six, he moved me, my stepmother, older sister and four brothers to a 53 acre farm in Glenwillow, Ohio.

Though it was in the country, our house was hardly a rural paradise. My father had built it on weekends while we still lived in Cleveland. It was constructed with concrete blocks and had only one large room, in which all eight of us lived. The house had no running water. Toilet facilities were an outhouse equipped with a year-old Montgomery Ward catalogue and a slop bucket for inside the house. The bed which I shared with my three younger brothers consisted of an uncovered mattress and a couple of moth-eaten blankets.

My father was the sort of man who believed you were old enough to work when you were old enough to walk. All of us kids had jobs, even my three-year-old brother Joe. Mine was cow-watcher, an operation which allowed my father to avoid the expense and work of building fences. Carrying a piece of rye bread for my breakfast, I'd take the cows out to pasture at 7:00, keep watch over them until noon, then bring them back, water them down and take them back out for the afternoon. Two or three times every summer, I'd fall asleep and the cows would head for the cornfield. I'd chase them out and frantically try to cover up the damage they had done. But there was no way to disguise two rows of chewed-up corn, so I'd spend the rest of the day in terror, waiting for my father to come home. Depending on how drunk he was and where he happened to catch me, I was beaten with anything from a razor strop to an ax handle.

My father was superstitious about many things, including left-handed people. He thought they were inherently inferior and stupid. Unfortunately, I was left-handed, and every time he spotted me using my left hand for writing or eating, I would get a beating.

Living on the farm was a very rough, almost primitive existence, especially because of the old man's brutality and because of the work he made us do. Things didn't improve much when I started going to school in Solon, a town of 5,000 people within commuting distance of Cleveland. It had an elite comprised of people who commuted to their professional jobs in Cleveland and lived in small enclaves of homes in exclusive areas with names like Briar Hill and Sherbrook Park. Their sons and daughters gave the Solon school system a college preparatory flavor and made me feel like one of those poor, dumb Meggyesy kids fresh off their run-down farm. This feeling of inferiority stayed with me throughout high school, and I know it stayed with my brothers. One of our prime motivations was to escape this feeling by achieving something big.

My first organized athletic experience was competing in track at Solon in the seventh and eighth grades. I was one of the smallest kids in my class and the coach assigned me to the mile run. In the few meets I ran in, I was one of the few milers ever to get lapped. The coach told us it was as important to finish the race as it was to win. I took his advice seriously, even though on more than one occasion it meant the humiliation of fighting my way through officials and runners preparing for the next race on my way to the finish line.

I began to play football in my sophomore year of high school. Practice for the Solon Comets began August 20, a few weeks before school opened. The assistant coach in charge of the backs was one of those crew-cut, drill instructor types—a real fanatic, always yelling, screaming, blowing his whistle and giving orders. On my first day out for the team, I didn't quite know what to do so I picked up cues from the more experienced guys.

I was doing jumping jacks in a leisurely way when this coach came over and began watching me. He didn't know my name, but he noticed the number on my jersey. "Hey there! You, number 63, get your ass moving!" he shouted. I was startled and pointed to my number, which I hadn't yet memorized. "Yes, you," he yelled. "Get your ass in gear if you want to make this football team." I began jumping furiously—and kept jumping in one way or another until I quit football 14 years later.

The most significant thing to me about football that first year was not playing the game itself but gaining the approval and respect of Head Coach Bob Vogt. Like the other kids, I would do anything on the football field that I thought would make him happy. I became a back because it was the best chance to make the team, but I only weighed 150 pounds and I wasn't very good. Still, I quickly gained the admiration of my teammates and Coach Vogt for my aggressive play. I was a real hustling fanatic once I stepped onto the football field. This was the first time I had ever received praise directly for anything I had done and I thrived on it. Football quickly became my life, and, in a pattern I was to see repeated time and again, the coach became a sort of substitute father. Vogt at times seemed to show a genuine concern, perhaps because he too had been poor and made it through college only with the help of a football scholarship. I remember driving with him once when he pointed out his boyhood home, a dilapidated old farmhouse much like my own. He didn't say anything except that he had lived there as a boy; but the implication was clear to me: football could be my ladder to a new life, and Coach Vogt would be the model for a new me.

I knew almost nothing about football but I did know I was playing for big stakes—my own survival. And, although I didn't develop any real football finesse until near the end of my junior year, right from the start my trademark was that I was an aggressive, hustling hitter.

I still remember my first scrimmage. I was so frantic to make the team and please Vogt that I couldn't think straight. The one play I remembered was a 44 dive where the linemen split guard and tackle and the halfback drove through. Near the end of the scrimmage, the quarterback called on me for a 44 dive five times in a row. I remember one of those five times vividly: I had gone about five yards past the line of scrimmage before I was hit by the linebacker; I carried him for five more yards when he grabbed hold of my helmet and ripped it off, but I spun loose and went for 15 more yards before finally going down. It was an excruciating pleasure, making that run. I looked over and noticed the varsity players just staring in amazement and pointing at me, and Coach Vogt nodding in approval.

I developed a style the coaches loved. The more approval they gave me, the more fanatically I played. From an early age, I had learned to endure violence and brutality as simply a part of my life. But in football, the brutality became legitimate, a way of being accepted on the football field and off.

My fanatical approach had its limits, though. I didn't play much because I got so hyped up I often couldn't remember the plays. Our first game my sophomore year was against Cuyahoga Heights, a pretty rough bunch of kids from a steel town on the west side. They didn't have much finesse; they simply beat the daylights out of their opponents. Russ Davis, our regular right halfback, was hurt, and Coach Vogt put me in the game. I freaked out, getting so excited I couldn't remember the plays except for my old standby, the 44 dive. I survived the first series because the quarterback stuck mainly to this play, but when he began to mix the plays up, it was all over. I was asking him in the huddle, "Where do I go on this one? What do I do?" He finally got mad and motioned to Coach Vogt, who quickly hustled me off the field.

Basketball practice began a week after the football season ended. I went out for the junior varsity team, which Bob Vogt also coached. As in football, I didn't have much finesse, but won a starting position on the basis of my brutal rebounding. I was the team's hatchet man, and the aggression expected of me on the football field spilled over to my play on the court. Once I remember coming down with a rebound and instinctively tucking it under my arm and running up court.

In the spring of my sophomore year I decided to leave Solon and go live with my uncle in Detroit. Things had really disintegrated at the farm. My older brother had gone into the Navy and my sister had left for Cleveland to get married. The old man was hitting the bottle heavily and he and my stepmother were about to get a divorce. I went to Coach Vogt for advice. We had a long talk in his office. He strongly suggested I stay in Solon since I had already established myself as an athlete, and told me I had shown enough promise as a sophomore to have a good chance of winning a college football scholarship in my senior year. As I was leaving his office he told me Mark Weber, the star of that year's team and a player he knew I greatly admired, had received a football scholarship to Syracuse and suggested I keep that in mind.

My friend and teammate, Bill Davidson, had also heard of my plans to move to Detroit, and, unknown to me, had approached his parents about the possibility of my moving in with them. Bill's father was an executive with General Electric and they lived in a secluded redwood ranch house in Briar Hill, the most exclusive residential section in Solon. I was to spend a week living with the Davidsons on a trial basis to see how we would get along. After one of Mrs. Davidson's meals, I was determined to be on my best behavior! Living there would be like moving from a pigpen to a palace. At the end of the week, they told me I could move in if it was all right with my parents. The old man had no objections, so I gathered all my belongings in a brown paper bag, said goodbye to my brothers, and left home.

When I went out for football practice the summer before my junior year, Coach Vogt switched me to tackle. I had grown a lot that summer but I'd also lost some of my speed and coordination. I had been living with the Davidsons for about three months by the time practice started, which meant eating three full meals a day for the first time in my life.

Adjusting to life at Briar Hill put me through a lot of mental changes. Not long after I moved in, Mrs. Davidson took me to a men's store in Cleveland and outfitted me in the style of the day—button-down shirts, V-neck sweaters, khaki pants, and loafers. This was quite a change from my J. C. Penney blue jeans and Montgomery Ward flannel shirts, and it confused the students at Solon: the poor, dumb Meggyesy kid was now dressing with class and sharing a Ford convertible with Bill Davidson.

I was a marginal man, as I would be for years to come, although the reasons changed. My new home and Ivy League clothes separated me from my old circle of friends, yet I wasn't fully accepted by the class-conscious Briar Hill kids. Even later when I developed into the star football player of Solon High, these people never accepted me as an equal, except on the athletic field.

I played tackle for most of my junior year and was having

a rather unspectacular season until the next to last game of the season against Cuyahoga Heights. We were down by two points going into the fourth quarter. Coach Vogt called quarterback Russ Keldorf and myself over to the sideline and told us he wanted me to switch to halfback. Since I was unfamiliar with the plays, Keldorf was instructed to stick to three basic plays, two of which had me carrying the ball. The field was muddy from a constant drizzle and when I went in at halfback we began to move for the first time that evening. With four minutes to go, we had worked down the field twice, only to have them stop us inside their twenty. Keldorf was calling my old standby, the 44 dive, most of the time, and I was picking up eight to ten yards at a crack, but we just couldn't get the ball into the end zone. With three minutes and 50 seconds to go, we began our last drive on our own 35 yard line. I carried the ball 12 times in a row and with 45 seconds to go we had first and goal to go on their three yard line. A touchdown would mean victory. By this time, though, the Cuyahoga Heights defense was keying on me, and the yardage was getting tough. Coach Vogt tried to be tricky, and sent in a play calling for a sweep by our other halfback. He was thrown for a yard loss. On second down another play came in from the bench—a pass to our tight end. It was nearly intercepted and fell incomplete. On third down, Vogt sent in my 44 dive. The hole was closed but I blasted my way down to the one yard line. I came back to the huddle really beat. It was fourth down with six seconds left on the clock. Vogt once again called for the 44 dive. Cuyahoga Heights had four men stacked in the hole and I could see them waiting for me. On the snap, instead of leveling my head and blasting in there, I hesitated, looked for an opening and attempted to pick my way through the pile. They nailed me and we lost the game.

I remember sitting by myself in a corner of the locker room, crying my head off. I felt it was my fault that we had lost the game. But even worse, I felt I had let Coach Vogt down. On my way into the locker room I had overheard him say to one of his assistants, "If he had hit in there like he did on third down, instead of trying to pussyfoot it over, he would have made it."

Looking back, the Cuyahoga Heights game was one of the many times in my football career when I saw clearly how corrupt the whole thing was and could have turned back—but decided to press on for reasons I didn't understand. I was really broken up, and I hoped Coach Vogt would say something to lessen my guilt. Instead he ignored me. Finally, I started to get angry. I thought, "I put out all this energy for a game and if it wasn't for me, it wouldn't even have been close." It was clear that Coach Vogt's prime concern was in winning football games and that he was concerned about his players only to the extent that they could contribute to that. He had been telling me for two years how much he cared about me as a person and I had believed him; but after I went all out to win a game and just barely failed, Vogt had no words for me. I never completely believed in coaches after that, although I wasn't quite able to step outside the father-son relationship that is football's cornerstone.

I also played basketball and ran track my junior year, but my participation in these sports was rather uneventful. I once again played the hatchetman role in basketball and ran the sprints and anchored the mile relay in track. Track was the most painful sport I have ever participated in. Our track coach had been a distance man in college, and he made the entire team, including sprinters, train like milers. Despite this, I liked track because it was the one sport where I got a chance to talk to athletes from other schools. In football these same guys were the faceless enemy, but in track we could lie around on the grass between events and rap. Track was a more natural sport—you could do what you had to do even though you were friendly with members of the other team.

Late in the spring just before school let out, I was elected football captain for the upcoming season. This made me feel directly responsible for the success of the team. Bill Davidson and I began serious training in July, a month before pre-season practice officially began. As captain, I wanted to build great *esprit de corps* among the players. In August, I had a party for the ball players at the Davidsons' to get the team together. We talked about what we had to do if we were going to be a winner that season. Our goal was the county championship.

By the time practice started on August 20, I weighed 195 pounds and had developed sprinter's speed. The first day of practice Coach Vogt put me at fullback, and in pre-season scrimmages I was just about unstoppable. I set a goal for myself to score at least one touchdown a game.

The first game was against North Royalton. Through the first three quarters, I was picking up good yardage. But despite all the yardage I had gained I hadn't been able to break loose for a touchdown. Then, early in the fourth quarter, the quarterback called a 32 trap. I shot through the hole, broke the linebacker's tackle and had only the safety between me and a touchdown. I had my balance and was running full speed. Just as the safety ducked his head to get me, I caught him with a forearm and ran over him for a 72 yard touchdown.

The season was off to a great start. We had won, and I had a good game. The next Monday, Coach Vogt called me out of study hall to talk with me. Standing in the hallway, he began to lay this rap on me about girls, school, and football. "There are three things a person can do when he is in high school," he began. "He can play football, he can study to keep his average up, or he can go out with girls. And you can't do more than two of these things well." I had never seen things this way and he could see the puzzled look on

---

Dave Meggyesy as a senior at Solon High in 1958.

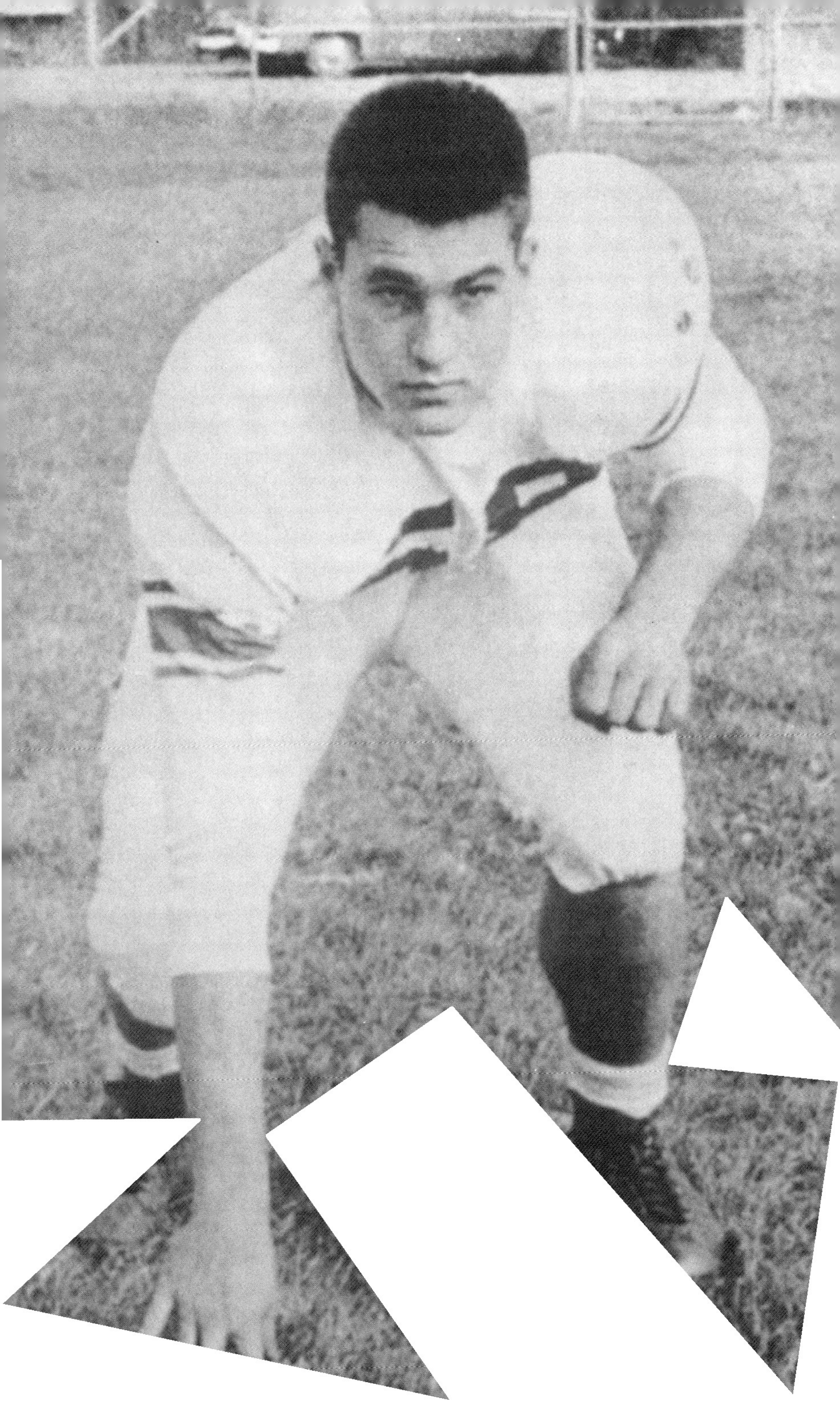

my face. He went on to tell me there was a "certain girl" in the school who had "destroyed" one of our top players the year before. I had just begun going out with her (she was one of Solon's cheerleaders and the toughest-looking girl in the school). In one way Coach Vogt and I had similar concerns: we were both worried about my getting together with this certain girl.

He also mentioned that I had a good future in football, and added that if I continued like I did in the first game I might get a scholarship to Syracuse, whose chief scout, Bill Bell, had picked up two former Solon High players: Roger Davis and Mark Weber. Vogt even told me a solid recommendation from him would guarantee me a scholarship to Syracuse. The implication was clear: if I played ball with Coach Vogt and not with this girl, I would be sure to get a scholarship to Syracuse. I complied.

This brief encounter was a good metaphor for the whole high school football ethic. The coach was not only concerned with football; consciously or unconsciously, he was trying to instill in us a particular view of the world. We were made to feel that, because we were football players, we were somehow superior. Vogt tried to get us to see ourselves as the "good people" in the school as opposed to the "bad people"—those who weren't submitting themselves to the system. He felt that as you became a better athlete you became a better person. Football represents the core values of the status quo, and coaches and school administrators want players to win adherents to these values, not only on the football field but also in their private lives.

As team captain, it was my responsibility to help get the guys psyched up for each game. Every Thursday afternoon, after the last practice session before the game, the team would meet on the practice field without the coaches. I'd give an impassioned speech on how we had to win the game for the school, Coach Vogt, and the whole coaching staff. I'd put a lot of stress on team pride, individual pride, and the tradition of good football at Solon High. I would point out that many people would be watching us and we had to show we were a good football team and that we weren't quitters. Then I'd go on to talk about one or two good players from the team we would face in Friday night's game and what strategy we should use to handle them. I'd stress to them how we had to obliterate everything from our minds except football between now and game time, so we would be mentally ready for the game. Finally, I would kneel down and the team would gather around me. We would all put our hands together. Then I'd say, "We're going to get them," and they'd scream, "Yeah." Then I'd holler, "OK, let's go get them," and we'd break out and head for the locker room feeling psyched up for the game.

Our games started at eight o'clock. At four-thirty, Bill Davidson and I would have our pre-game meal. We always ate the exact same thing: a cup of tea with four spoonfuls of sugar and some mashed up broiled hamburger on a piece of toast. Dick Clark's rock and roll show was always on at this time, so we would watch it on the tube and hope he played a lot of heavy rock music to help us get psyched up. A little after six we'd leave for a special service at the Solon Presbyterian Church. Rev. Bill Drake, a former college athlete, would give a short inspirational talk and lead us in prayer. We'd leave the church ready for a battle that by that time seemed like the final contest between good and evil.

At the stadium, we'd get our ankles taped, put on our uniforms, and then lie around the locker room looking very solemn. Except for Coach Vogt's pep talk the locker room resembled a funeral parlor. We all felt somewhat uncomfortable and were anxious to get out of it. We had to walk about 60 yards from the locker room to the big chain link fence surrounding the playing field as the fans were flowing in. At the gate to the field the guys would gather around me and I'd say, "We're really going to win tonight, it's a crucial game. I know everybody is ready to play." And then I'd say "We're going to get them," and they'd answer "Yeah!" We'd repeat this four or five times until we really got ourselves going and then, boom, the gate would fly open, we'd burst through and run single file around the field.

Since we only had 26 guys we would really spread ourselves out when doing our pre-game lap around the field. I remember the time we were playing Mayfield High

School, which came to Solon with a herd of about 60 guys. They looked like an army when they paraded around the field and did their calisthenics. I remember saying to myself while warming up, "I don't know about this game." I was really swallowing it. It was near the end of the season, and I was being touted as the best fullback in the county. They kicked off, and on the first play from scrimmage I went through on a quick hitter off tackle. I was met at the line of scrimmage by their linebacker and their tackle Darryl Sanders, who later starred at Ohio State and with the Detroit Lions. They really put it to me, and as they were getting up the linebacker said, "Meggyesy, you're not so tough." I knew then it was going to be a long night. I managed to gain over 100 yards, but for the first time in my life I began to experience fear on the playing field. The fears kept creeping in and for a while I could hardly control them. I began to question the brutality of the game—these guys on the other side of the line were obviously trying to smash the hell out of me.

I learned a lot more about pain the first time I ever played with a serious injury. That was the Warrensville game my senior year. On the Tuesday before the game, Coach Vogt had us doing this drill we called "ground-hogging." Two players would get down on their hands and knees facing each other—you could only use your head and had to keep your hands and knees on the ground. The object of the drill was to butt the other player on his back, and the lower you got to the ground the better leverage you had for tipping him over. During this drill I injured my neck so badly that the next morning I couldn't move my head—it was stuck over to one side. I went to the doctor that afternoon and he diagnosed it as a "wry neck." He told me not to practice for the rest of the week and to come back on Friday. My neck had not improved by Friday morning, but when Coach Vogt saw me at school, he said he hoped I would be ready for the game that night. I was anxious to play, too, for it was a big game and I had never missed a game because of an injury.

I went to the doctor Friday afternoon before the game. He stuck a long needle into the big muscle knot in my neck. When he tried to pull the needle out, the muscle spasmed. The needle broke from the base of the syringe and I was left with it sticking in my neck. The doctor took a pair of pliers out of the drawer and pulled it out. Mrs. Davidson had brought me to the office, and when she saw this, she turned very pale and I thought she was going to pass out. I was so spaced out about playing, though, it didn't matter at all to me. I didn't realize it, but he was shooting me up with Novocaine for the game. He assured me everything would be all right, and sure enough much of the pain was gone by the time I left his office. I still couldn't move my neck, but I was happy it didn't hurt any more.

Coach Vogt used me only on third downs during the first

half of the game. When we came out for the second half we were down by 14 points, and Vogt began putting me in on second down situations and keeping me in for two or three plays. By the fourth quarter we were still behind, and Vogt now had me on the field for just about all the offensive plays. We moved the ball well and scored a few touchdowns. However, we couldn't contain them at all on defense and we lost the game.

When the numbness wore off after the game, my head felt like it was on backwards. But even though the pain in my neck kept getting worse as the drug wore off, I was required to go to the post-game party with all of the other players. Coach Vogt started these gatherings for both teams in my junior year. They were hosted by the owner of a local restaurant, and most of us made an appearance only because we were required to. It seemed stupid; Vogt had been getting us psyched up all week to beat our opponents, and then he expected us to sit down and be friendly over Cokes and hotdogs after we battled them for two hours on the playing field.

The business of setting up a dividing line between us and our opponents went on the whole week before a game. Vogt would call Chagrin Falls, our big rival, "the boys from across the river," and Mayfield was a team of "dumb but tough Wops." And at the beginning of the game I would give my "We've got to get them, we've got to get them" speech. We were really fired up and felt we were going to annihilate "them." I particularly didn't want to see their faces, because the more anonymous they were the better it was for me—and I'm sure most of the other ball players felt the same way: they were a faceless enemy we had to meet.

■Meggyesy met many another faceless enemy before he quit football. Although he sometimes recognized the darker side of the sport, football was still the most important thing in his life.

As his coach had promised, he was offered a football scholarship from Syracuse University. At Syracuse he occasionally broke out of the mold that had been set for football players. He insisted on choosing his own courses (other players let assistant coaches fill out their course cards), and he insisted on associating with friends outside the narrow circle of other athletes. But he was still a gung-ho player, and when college was over he was picked by the St. Louis Cardinals in an early round of the annual professional draft of college players.

It wasn't until he had played five seasons with the Cardinals that he finally divorced himself from football. By then he was appalled by "what football does to those who play it."

The values of football—competitive spirit, aggressiveness, ability to resist pain—are not so different from those of other sports. Dave Meggyesy's rejection of them is particularly sobering because he spent so long in the game and received so much from it.

Don Schollander
WHO OWNS A CHAMPION?

■Few athletes have the talent and drive to become champions in their sport. Those who do often discover that the recognition they receive hardly makes up for the strain of being a public figure. A champion's life is not completely his own—he belongs to the public as well. And pleasing the public is an exhausting and demanding job.

Don Schollander became a champion swimmer. He began swimming seriously at 9 and left his home in Oregon at 15 to train under a top coach in Santa Clara, California. Within two years he was winning medals at national swimming competitions (the Nationals) and setting new world records. In 1964 he qualified for the U.S. Olympic swimming team. He was 18 years old and had just graduated from high school, but as a

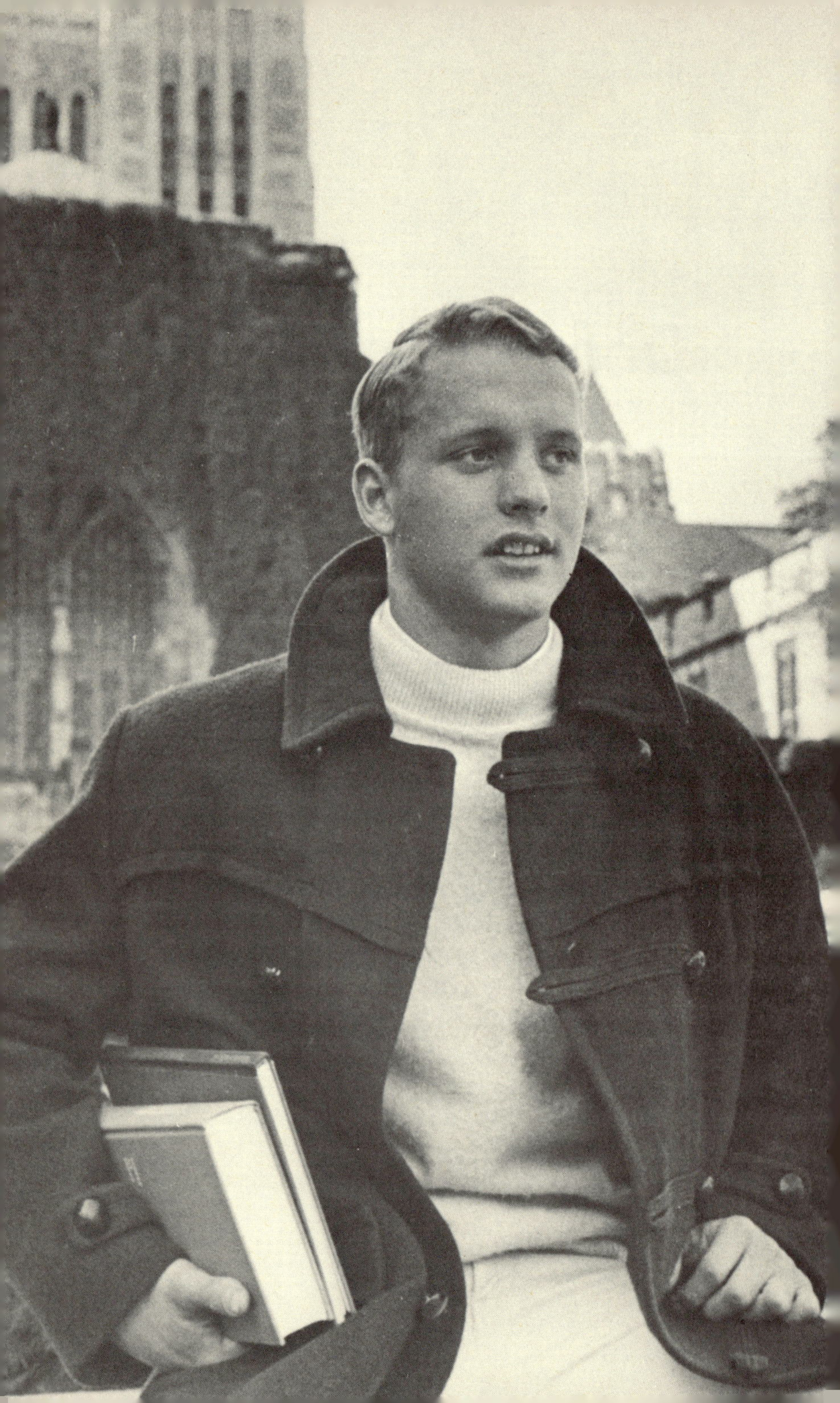

swimmer he was near his peak.

At the Olympics in Tokyo, Schollander won four gold medals—then an unprecedented feat for a swimmer. He was clearly the most admired and publicized participant in the Games. In a few short days of competition he had become an international celebrity. His picture appeared on the covers of many leading American magazines. He was featured in a film called *The Boy Who Swims Like a Fish*. He received dozens of awards and spoke at scores of banquets.

Becoming a celebrity would be difficult at any age, but it was particularly difficult at 18. Although Schollander wanted to continue swimming competitively, he also had other things to do. In January of 1965 he entered Yale University as a freshman. There, he thought, he could be a normal college student and continue to swim for the college team. It was not that simple. He still had responsibilities as a champion. In the following excerpt from his book *Deep Water* (written with a college roommate, Duke Savage), he tells what happened in the six months after he arrived at Yale.

Don Schollander at Yale in 1965.

WHO OWNS A CHAMPION?

I wanted Yale to be the beginning of something new, not just another stage in my swimming career. People were saying that Yale had accepted me only because of my swimming but that wasn't true. The acceptance came in April, 1964—before the Olympics and before the Nationals. There were no gold medals then shining up from my application.

I had heard so much about athletes who reached the top so young and then had nowhere to go. Many athletes are finished young, and then so many just hang on, living in the past. It's bad enough when this happens to a baseball or football player at thirty-five, but if I let it happen to me, I would be a "has-been"—over the hill—at twenty-two, if not sooner. I didn't intend to spend the next forty years—or the next four years—reliving the glory of two weeks in Tokyo.

On the trip from Kennedy Airport to New Haven that cold winter evening, I sat in the back seat of the airport limousine and thought about all this—that I wanted college to be the beginning of something new, that I was coming to Yale as a student, not as a swimmer, and that I hoped other people would see it that way, too.

In New Haven the car pulled to a stop at the Taft Hotel and another student and I climbed out and got our luggage.

He was coming in from Ireland and it turned out that we lived in the same freshman house—Welsh. For him it was a place; for me it was only an address.

We walked through Phelp's Gate and turned in front of Welsh Hall. "Here's where I get off," he said, at his entryway. "So long."

I walked up a flight of stairs, knocked on the door of room ninety-eight, and met my roommate. A tall guy with dark hair, thin face, strong jaw, a swimmer's broad shoulders. Barry Wemple. He had been a swimmer at Williston Academy Prep School and was on the Yale freshman team.

"Yeah, come on in," Wemple said and walked back to his desk. Then he pointed to a pile of boxes in a corner of the room. "There's your mail. I've been saving it for you."

The room was nearly empty—just Wemple's desk and chair, a couch, a beachcomber's chair and a small table. Through an open door I saw a very small bedroom with only one bed. I looked around a minute and asked Wemple if there was someplace I could get a bed.

"Oh, yeah. I had the janitor haul it away last September. I figured it would only be in the way. I'd have had it brought back but I didn't know you were coming so soon." Tonight, Wemple said, I could sleep on the couch.

"Okay," I said. "Then how do I get the bed back?"

"You can catch the janitor tomorrow."

I wanted my roommate to treat me like any other guy. I had hoped he wouldn't make a big thing of my Olympic success—and Barry Wemple sure wasn't making much of it.

The next day I got the bed into the room and took off for Germany to receive an award from the Association of International Sports Correspondents. Actually Barry Wemple was a hell of a nice guy, and we were good friends for our whole four years at Yale. But when you first meet him he's very cold; he doesn't knock himself out being friendly.

That first year at Yale was tough. Any hopes I'd had of being accepted as just another student, like anyone else, quickly vanished. This is something that most people starting out at college never think about. Why would they? What does it mean, after all, at college to be accepted like everyone else? It means being an unknown quantity. It means meeting people and wondering who they are and where they come from and what they are like—and going through a process of exploration to find out.

At Yale there were about eight thousand guys—every race, religion, nationality, every ethnic and economic background, every philosophy—and any one could meet any other one of the eight thousand and wonder what he was like, where he was going, and what he was all about. Except me.

I soon found out that I was the one man on campus who was different. Everybody knew me. They knew where I came from and what I did and they were pretty sure they knew all there was to know about me. Probably every guy on that campus still expected to prove himself in his chosen field. My field was settled. I had been there. I had nowhere else to go. I had a label: swimmer.

I had hoped to go unnoticed. Within a few days I began to feel like a campus monument. Everywhere I went people stared at me. Guys would point me out to each other or to their dates. I would look away and try not to be self-conscious about it, but when I looked back they would still be staring.

When I passed a group of people, before I was out of earshot, I would hear the whispers. Sometimes I would only make out my name, sometimes a few cynical remarks. In the co-op I overheard, "Schollander is no different from you and me. He gets up in the morning, brushes his teeth, eats his breakfast, and then goes to the swimming pool for the day."

In the Commons—the freshman dining hall—people would stare at me while I ate. I would sit there, usually alone because I hadn't had time to make friends yet, and I would be painfully aware that four or five guys at a nearby table were obviously discussing me. Not knowing anybody is hard enough, but when people have read about you in *Time*, *Sports Illustrated*, *The New York Times*, the *Yale Daily News*, and have seen your picture on the cover of *Life*, and when you're sitting there all alone with no one to talk to while they stare at you, it can be pretty miserable. Especially when you're a freshman at college and starting late and only eighteen.

Almost from the start I began to get hate letters, wishing me a short, unhappy stay at Yale. Little kids telephoned me and I would talk to them for a minute, but some of them kept calling me for four years. High-school girls called and offered to come over to see me—offered openly their services in bed. Homosexuals telephoned me. They would breathe over the phone about my nice body and then ask me to come over for a drink. That really shook me. After a while I realized that half of them were serious and the other half were playing sick jokes.

On top of everything else, the movie *The Boy Who Swims Like a Fish* was a co-feature at a downtown theatre.

My biggest problem was time. Even before classes began, the rat race started again. I returned from Germany on January 13, spent one night in New Haven, and took off again the next day for a pair of engagements in Ohio—a Touchdown Club dinner in Columbus and a National Swimming Institute dinner in Cleveland. Back in New Haven, I actually had a few free days to begin to find my way around Yale. The other guys were all taking exams, which only reminded me that I was still an outsider, starting college one semester late. But on January 21 I went to New York to tape "To Tell the Truth." Then I returned to New Haven, and three days later went back to New York—as guest of honor at the B'nai B'rith sportsmen's dinner. Then back to New Haven.

On February 1, classes began and I found myself taking sophomore courses. Most freshman courses were full year courses that couldn't be started in the second semester. The dean advised me to take five sophomore courses and make up my freshman requirements the following year, a decision that left me less than overjoyed because I'd already figured I'd be in for some academic troubles, coming in new this way in the second semester.

In my first small discussion class—most courses were large lecture courses—the professor helped these fears along. First he had trouble getting my name straight; then he wanted to know what I was doing there; then he needled me a while for not knowing some work that had been covered during the first semester; and finally he told me that he really didn't think I could keep up with a sophomore class.

A week after classes began, I was traveling again. On February 8, I went back to Oregon for "Don Schollander Day," which involved addressing a joint session of the state legislature and attending a reception afterward.

I came back to Yale on February 9, and five days later, on February 14, I went to Milwaukee to formally receive the Associated Press Top Male Athlete of the Year award.

A week later, on February 21, at the New York Athletic Club, I received another honor—the AAU Sullivan Award, which is given each year to "the amateur athlete who, by performance, example and good influence, did the most to advance the cause of good sportsmanship during the year." For this award not only sportswriters and sportscasters cast ballots, but also amateur sportsmen, including Olympic athletes.

On February 27, I was back in Oregon, this time to open the State Easter Seals campaign, of which I was honorary chairman. Back to Yale on the first of March.

On March 11, I was named winner of the first annual ABC–*Sports Illustrated* Grand Award of Sports. I was selected over such competition as pro-football star Jimmy Brown, all-American basketball star Bill Bradley, and Notre Dame football quarterback John Huarte.

With every passing week, time was becoming a more serious problem. I had a scholarship job in the Yale news bureau, where I spent two hours, five afternoons a week, writing to hometown newspapers about their local students at Yale. Then, every day at five o'clock I had swimming practice. I was managing to study about four or five hours a day, whereas other freshmen were averaging seven or eight hours.

When I did have a few hours to study I was constantly interrupted—not only by those nut calls from kids, girls, and sick jokesters, but by what seemed to be the entire working press of the East Coast. Yale officials had asked me—as part of their "town-gown" goodwill effort—to give special consideration to the local press and to speak at local high schools if I was invited to do so. And I did. But it was much more than the local press. It seemed as though, when I got to Yale, every magazine and newspaper that had been too far away to call me in Oregon decided to reach me in New Haven.

I was falling far behind in my studies. Anyone else with my schedule would have depended on weekends to catch up, but I was never there on weekends. I would be off somewhere getting an award.

I'd get back Sunday night and stay up late to study, go to four classes Monday morning and then collect the pile of mail that arrived in my box every day. I'd spend nearly an hour trying to separate the important letters or letters from friends from the fan letters and the hate letters. I began to consider a fan letter an imposition because I had to give two minutes that I couldn't spare to anwering it. The evenings were mine, except for Wednesday, when there was usually a swimming meet, and weekends when I was usually away. Evenings I studied, trying to accomplish in three hours what most guys were doing in eight. By eleven most of the guys would start to hack around, and I wanted to hack around, too, and try to make some friends, which I wasn't doing because I had to study. Then it would be Friday and I'd be off again on the banquet circuit.

I didn't have many dates my freshman year. On the few weekends I stayed in New Haven I used to walk across the campus around midnight after the library closed. I would see all the guys walking with girls or hear the music coming from some party. I used to look forward to the weekends I could spend at Yale but then I would get so depressed. I realized that I wasn't having any fun at college.

Invitations began to arrive from almost every country in Europe, asking me to visit during the summer. Ordinarily I would have been thrilled, but as they piled up, along with the American invitations, the summer just began to look like an extension of the nightmare.

If I was a marked and pressured man on campus it was worse in the pool. I was swimming regularly on the Yale freshman team and I kept telling myself that I ought to get into condition, but I never had the time. I would turn up at a meet and swim my events—almost mechanically. I never thought about the race in advance. I always had too much work; I was always running; I was always tired.

My attitude toward swimming was changing, a fact that hit home suddenly at a minor meet with a prep school—Williston. I'd been so busy I hadn't thought much about the race ahead of time, but when I got to the pool that Saturday afternoon, I saw that the stadium was jammed. The reason for the excitement was one very good swimmer on the Williston team, Jim Edwards, who had just missed making the Olympics in the 100-meter. Suddenly it hit me: first, I was terribly out of condition, and, also, I might actually *lose* to a prep-school swimmer in front of a packed stadium. Yale would win the meet by thirty or forty points anyway; the team victory was not at stake. Nothing was at stake—except my pride and my record. For the first time I swam for no other reason, no other goal, except *not to lose*.

Before the race I did everything I could to psyche that guy out; I put on a great show of confidence. Swimming the race I gave it everything I had. And I just barely touched him out. I won on my reputation, really, and I knew it. Edwards was afraid to pull too far ahead of me too early in the race.

That night, alone, I walked around the old campus for a long time and thought about how my life had changed and how I had changed. For years—all those years, as far back as I could remember—I swam to win. Because I loved to win. And I had always believed that was one of the reasons I won—because I swam to win. Now I was swimming only *not to lose*.

The Harvard meet was scheduled for March 13 in Cambridge. For at least a month before it I'd heard about Bill Shrout, a Harvard freshman who had gone undefeated all season. And I'd heard, too, that Harvard fans were just waiting to see what he could do against me. Bill Shrout at Harvard was Jim Edwards at Williston all over again—only worse. And I was worse. I still hadn't had time to get into condition. I was away every weekend in February, and I was falling even farther behind in my work. And more and more I was aware of the long line of guys, psyched-up and in peak condition, just waiting to knock me off. Shrout at

Harvard was next in line for his turn at bat.

Some time before the day of the meet I had to turn out two papers that were due the following Monday and study for a one hour test scheduled for that same Monday. I was really pushing the work and couldn't even think about psyching myself up for a race. At one point during the week before that meet I was suddenly so overwhelmed by the work load and so frustrated by my own fatigue that I didn't see how I could swim at all. I really felt I was going to lose. Five months earlier I'd been a champion—on top of the world. Now I felt I couldn't cope any longer with the pressures and confusion that championship had brought.

The stadium at Harvard was packed with a noisy, excited crowd. A kind of fever had built up about this meeting between Shrout and me. The Boston sportswriters had played up the freshman meet over the varsity meet. A television station was covering the freshman meet only. The public loves an underdog, and there was real excitement in the prospect that undefeated Bill Shrout might knock me down. For me, I had changed public roles quickly and the new one of a Goliath whom people were waiting to see get it right between the eyes was not a very happy one. And yet I knew it was true. Ninety percent of that crowd wanted to see me get killed.

All winter I had been swimming mostly the 100 and the 200. Shrout had been swimming the 200 and the 500. Now Jim Barton, the Yale freshman coach, asked me to go up to

Shrout's distances for the Harvard meet and swim the 200 and the 500. I agreed to do it. What else could I do? The reason for all the excitement—the only reason the meet was being televised—was that I was supposed to be meeting Shrout. Again I had the feeling of being swept along by public demands against which there was no protection and little I could do.

The whole meet turned out to be a hideous mix-up. The usual practice at these meets is not to submit names in advance but to announce the contestants in each race just before it begins. When the 200 was announced, I was in it and Shrout was not. I thought maybe he was avoiding me in the 200, which has always been considered my best race, to go after me in the 500. He probably knew that I wasn't in any kind of shape for an endurance race. I could sense the disappointment in the crowd so I tried to swim a good race—to give them something. I set a new NCAA freshman record for the 200, but actually it wasn't much of a record and I didn't have to go all out to do it.

Next came the 50-yard freestyle. Shrout was in that. I was not. I hadn't swum a 50-yard race in years. The crowd grumbled, there was talk that I was avoiding Shrout. Shrout swam his 50-yard race and he won. Then came some diving events and some other swimming events.

Then the 100 free. Again Shrout was in it and I was not. To me it was clear what had happened. The Harvard coach had figured I would swim the 100 and Shrout had dropped down to my event; Jim Barton had asked me to go up to the 200 and the 500, even though I hadn't done them all year, because they were Shrout's usual events. The crowd understood none of this. They only knew that once again I was not going to meet Shrout and they started to boo me. At first there were a few scattered boos and hisses and then more and more people picked it up. For a few minutes the race was delayed because of all the commotion in the stadium. Then, at last, the crowd calmed down and Shrout won the 100 free easily and got a roaring ovation.

I felt badly about the mix-up, so when the 500 free came up I tried first to make it a close, exciting race—to pull the other swimmers with me. When I saw I couldn't give them a close race, I tried to swim as beautifully as I could. Nobody was interested. Finally I decided to swim as fast as I could. I really knocked myself out and I broke another NCAA record and received some polite applause, mostly from the Yale people in the crowd.

When I pulled myself out of the pool after the 500, I noticed a slight twitching in my arms. This had never happened to me before. I had been tired after races, but never so tired that the muscles in my limbs started to give out. It wasn't a serious twitching, but it betrayed more than normal fatigue, even after a long race. For a minute I was puzzled. I looked at the twitching and thought, That's

---

Don Schollander competing in 1966.

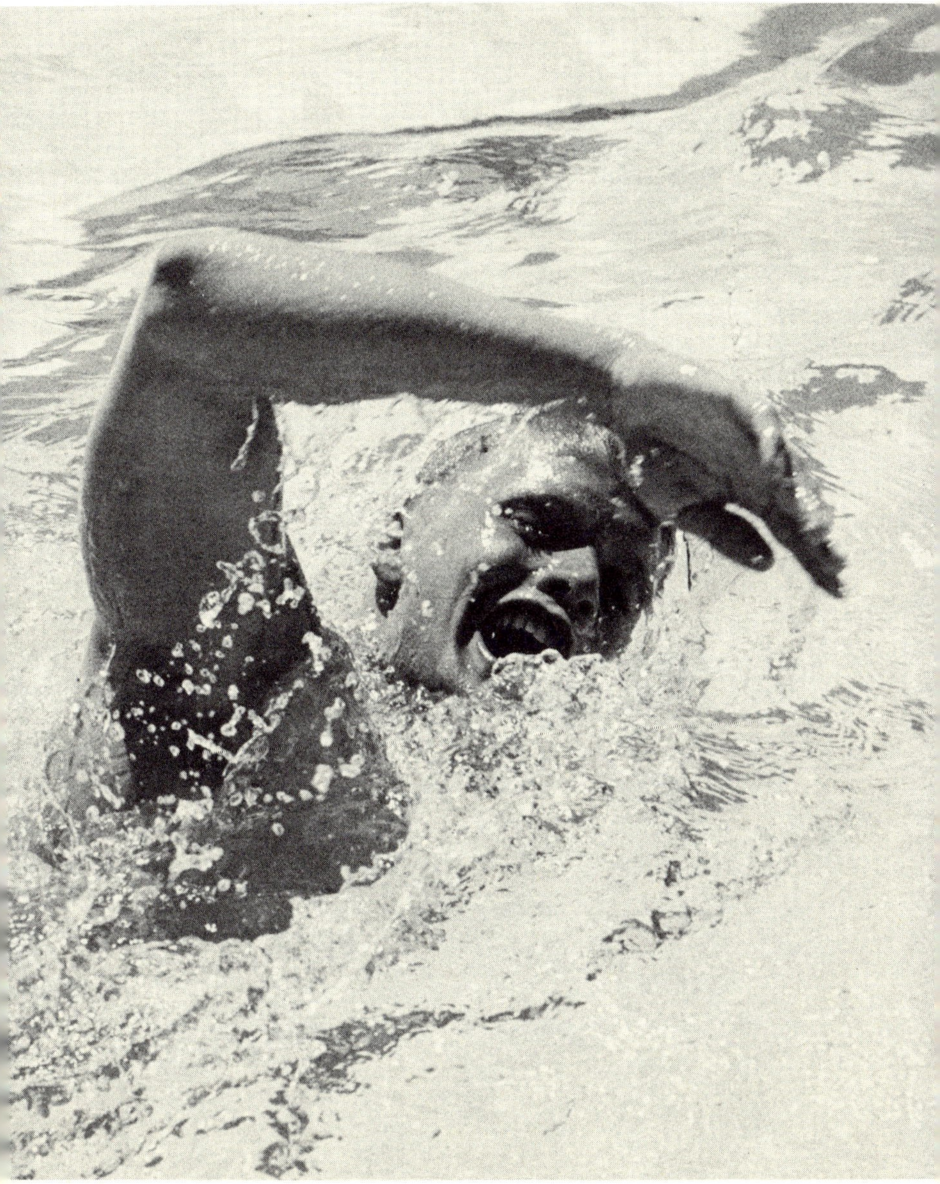

strange, and then I forgot about it.

The final event of the meet, just two events after the 500, was the 4 x 100 freestyle relay. Even in top condition I wouldn't have been entered after swimming 500 yards only ten minutes earlier. I was glad that for me the meet was over. I had really gone all out to break that record and I was exhausted.

But after the 500 Jim Barton asked me to swim the anchor leg of the relay because Shrout was swimming it for Harvard. I thought he was joking.

"Yeah, right," I said.

"I'm serious," he said.

I couldn't believe it! Shrout had been resting for five long events—at least half an hour—and I had just gotten out of the pool after swimming 500 yards. And during the entire afternoon Shrout had swum a total of 150 yards (50 plus 100), while I had swum 700 yards (200 plus 500). I told Jim that Shrout would kill me if I tried to do that anchor leg. By now some of the Yale varsity swimmers were coming out of the locker room and they couldn't believe that I was being asked to swim the anchor leg of a relay ten minutes after swimming the 500 free. A couple of them even said, "Jim, are you kidding?"

But Jim was serious, and in a way I knew how he felt. He was a rookie coach—this was his first year at Yale—and this was an important meet. A lot of fever had built up, and probably he felt that he should have straightened out the races ahead of time. At any rate, he pressed me to swim the relay and finally I agreed. Also I guess I didn't like the idea of people booing me and saying I had ducked meeting Shrout.

I hoped I would go out either way ahead of Shrout or so far behind him that I couldn't be expected to catch up—in a close race, I knew, he would murder me.

We went out almost together; I had a small lead of about a yard. By the 50-yard wall he had closed it and we were together. On the third lap he went ahead. I knew he was going to outsplit me; I was just trying to hang onto the race for Yale. Until the final turn I just held in there, trying not to fall too far behind. Then, on the last 25 yards I pulled out everything I had left in me and managed one final spurt. It was enough to catch up and just touch him out to win.

He had outsplit me—by a fraction of a second. When they announced the split times the Harvard fans went wild. I hardly heard it. All I could think of at the end of that race was how tired I was.

A week later vacation began and all I wanted to do was rest. I thought how great it would be to just go somewhere and sleep in the sun. I'd have been happy just to go home to Oregon and sleep for a week. But I spent the vacation in New Haven. I had a couple of speaking engagements in the East and I had a lot of work to catch up on—and the Spring Nationals were to be held at Yale on April 1 to 3, during the last few days of vacation. Also *Life* was sending a reporter and a photographer to New Haven to do a story on me. They wanted to cover me at the Nationals and then through a few days of "life at Yale" after classes started again on April 5.

Those 1965 Spring Nationals were the most frantic I remember. I'd asked Patience Sherman to come up to visit me and I was damn glad to see her. At that point I needed a date and a good friend and Patience was both. But the days of careful peaking—a regular schedule, plenty of rest, no diversion, no wasted energy—were gone. All through the Nationals I was entertaining the reporter and photographer from *Life*; even when they are the nicest guys in the world, this takes a lot of time. They are there to get a story, and they put in a full day's work every day.

The *Life* reporter and photographer followed me wherever I went. They came to my room at seven in the morning and took pictures of me getting dressed. They took pictures of me eating, swimming, racing. After school began, they came to classes with me and to the dining room. I was flattered that *Life* wanted to do a whole article on me, but having these guys taking pictures of me all over the campus was embarrassing.

For the Spring Nationals I was entered in three relays and the 200-yard freestyle, in which I managed to set a new indoor record. After that race a couple of people said that I had all the conditioning and the style and the power that had brought me four gold medals in Tokyo. But I knew better. I was tired. I was tired all the time now.

By mid-April I felt I had reached rock bottom. Physically I felt rotten. And no matter what I did, I couldn't catch up on the work. With exams just a month away I was actually afraid I might flunk out. I was turning down all new invitations now but my schedule was still cluttered with old promises. In April I had to reopen the World's Fair in New York. On May 3 I was due in New York again to receive the National Academy of Sports Award.

My last exam was in sociology, and I stayed up all night studying for it. At five in the morning I remember I was looking out the window, watching the sun come up over the old campus. I stood there thinking about all the things the old campus was supposed to mean to a freshman—things I had missed: touch football in the fall, snowball fights in the winter, stickball in the spring, the freshmen riot held every year on the first Thursday in May. I was at a banquet in New York the night of the first Thursday in May. I thought about all the friends you made on the old campus before your class split up and went into residential colleges. I thought that morning about the "road trips" to Smith and Vassar I had had to turn down to study or to go somewhere and make a speech, and about the bull sessions over coffee after dinner I had had to pass up because I just didn't have time. Next year, I thought, somehow I would get on top of all this. Next year when I came back to Yale, I would settle in as a student. I wouldn't be transient again.

A few days later, on June 8, I went to the White House to a reception given by President Johnson for the presidential scholars—the outstanding high-school seniors from all fifty states. Famous people in many different fields had been invited so that the students could talk to them. And I was supposed to be one of the famous people they might like to talk to. I talked most of the time to John Glenn, and I kept thinking that I was only a year older than the students and that I really belonged on the other side of the fence. I was really one of the kids, interested in talking to these important people.

The next day I went home to Oregon. I was still going to Europe but I had stayed firm in my decision to limit my trip to three countries, Germany, Switzerland, and Belgium. I could have left from New York, and I should have, but months earlier I had promised to be the grand marshal of the Portland Rose Festival, the biggest event of the year to the people in Oregon, which was to begin on June 12. So I went six thousand miles out of my way to be in a parade. For the first time in my life I slept on a plane. And when I got home all I wanted to do was sleep.

I landed in Würzburg on the sixteenth and went right to sleep. I was scheduled to compete against Hans Klein the next night. In January I had told Hans that I wouldn't be in condition to race against him in this meet. He had laughed and said, "Neither will I; neither will I! We'll probably swim the slowest race in history." But he was in condition and he beat me—badly.

After the race Hans came into the locker room, really upset. He didn't want me to think it was a setup. He said he hadn't really trained for this meet; he hadn't expected me to be in such terrible shape. I told Hans I thought I was sick and he agreed there must be something wrong with me. But what could Hans do?

By the time I reached Switzerland I felt rotten. I spent the whole first day in bed, resting. The second day I worked out a little and then joined the rest of the party on a trip up into the nearby Alps. I've always loved mountains and this was something I really wanted to see. We drove part of the way up into the mountains and then took the chairlift to the top and walked to the very summit. It was one of the most beautiful days I've ever seen—and one of the most magnificent views. But when we got home that night I was so tired I couldn't believe it. In the morning I asked to see a doctor.

In Berne a doctor examined me and said that I was probably coming down with a cold. But by now I knew that my rate of recovery after a swim was too slow, which indicated an infection, and I insisted that there *was* something wrong with me. The doctor insisted there was not. I told the people promoting the race that I was too sick to swim. They took me to a specialist who assured me that I was well enough to swim. I was beginning to suspect that I might have mononucleosis, but the doctor said I didn't have mononucleosis. The promoters pointed out that they had an investment in me and it was my duty to swim since two doctors had assured me there was nothing wrong with me.

So I swam. I swam 200 meters in two minutes, seven seconds, ten seconds slower than my normal time. I still came in first because in Switzerland swimming is not a major sport. Then after the race, I tried to pull myself out of the pool and could not. I tried again. I got halfway up and then my arms gave out and I slipped back into the water. I just hung onto the edge until a couple of people pulled me out. They rushed me to the hospital.

My world was very quiet at last.

When I woke up in the hospital the next morning, a doctor told me that I had glandular fever, which is the European term for mononucleosis. I thought, Good, and rolled over and went back to sleep. For four or five days I lay there; I remember thinking, in the rare moments when I was awake, how good it felt just to lie in that bed and sleep and not have to catch any planes or answer any telephones or make any speeches or swim any races. Nobody was asking me to do anything.

For four or five days my condition grew worse. My temperature went as high as 104 and the drugs didn't seem to affect it. The doctor suspected that hepatitis was setting in. That scared me. I knew that hepatitis was a common but dangerous complication of mononucleosis, and that people died of hepatitis. At that point the AAU got concerned and considered sending a man over to look into what had happened. My father made reservations to fly over. Then my fever broke and the AAU stayed home and my father stayed home and I was okay. I simply woke up one morning feeling fine. Obviously one of the drugs had worked, but I remember thinking, Hell, all I needed was a little sleep—because once I got it I felt great.

By the time I could sit up and read I had hundreds of letters and telegrams from all over—Europe, America, Japan. This was the good side of being a world figure. Of all of them I remember one from my old friend Carolyn Wood of Portland: "Dear Don—America just honors its heroes to the point of destruction."

■After a long rest Schollander did return to swimming. And he returned to Yale, learning to balance the demands of swimming with the demands of college. In June of 1968 he went through graduation ceremonies with his class at Yale although he still had one semester of work to make up. Then he went into last-minute training for the summer Olympics at Mexico City.

He won two gold medals at Mexico City, a fine accomplishment for an "old" swimmer of 22, and a fitting ending to his life as a competitive athlete. One of his teammates at the 1968 Games was a younger swimmer named Mark Spitz, who would set a new record in 1972 by winning seven gold medals. Like Schollander, Spitz became a national figure and in turn faced the demands put on a sports celebrity.

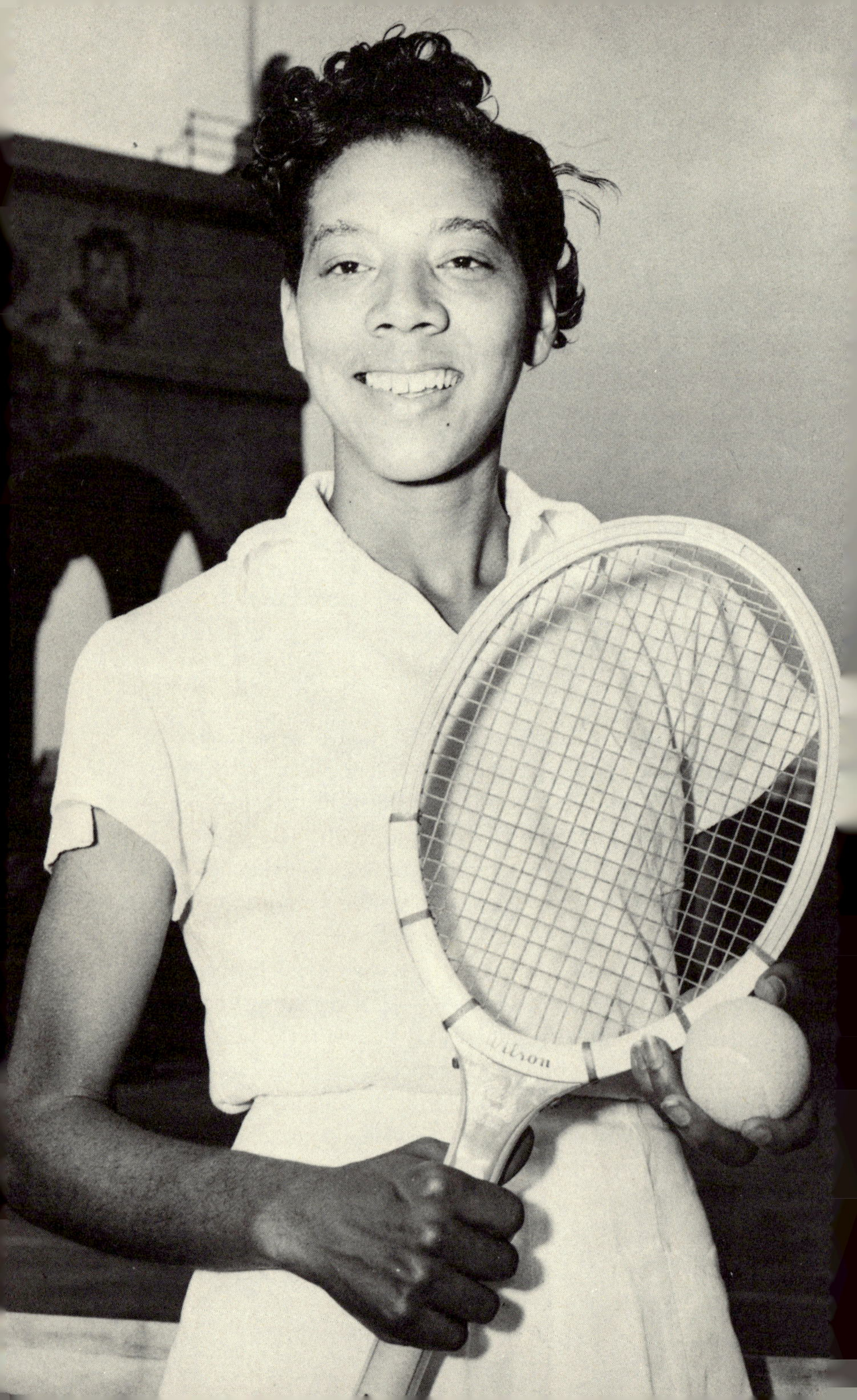

Althea Gibson
AN AMAZINGLY GENEROUS THING

■Most young athletes need help to break into their chosen sport, and some need more than others. We have already seen that Spencer Haywood's brother got him a start in organized basketball, that his coach became his legal guardian and adviser, and that a family in Detroit took him in as a son. Dave Meggyesy also received special help from a family.

Althea Gibson grew up on the streets of Harlem. In 1941, when she was 14, she had run away from home, dropped out of school, found and then lost a job. She lived on a small allowance from the welfare department and boarded with a

Althea Gibson at Forest Hills in 1950, a few days before she competed in the Nationals there.

foster family. She was a good bowler and a great two-on-two basketball player, but these skills didn't promise a very bright future.

Then she discovered tennis. Soon she was the best black woman player in America. In her early twenties she became the first black player to compete in many national and international tournaments. At a time when black athletic stars were rare, she integrated tennis and achieved worldwide fame.

Althea's success was all the more remarkable because tennis was then traditionally reserved for the rich and socially prominent. Her career took her far from the streets of Harlem. From her earliest days, she had shown the grit and competitive fire that could make her great. But to succeed in this sport of the wealthy she needed more help than most, both on and off the tennis court. In her autobiography, *I Always Wanted To Be Somebody* (written with Edward E. Fitzgerald), she acknowledges the many people—friends, fans, coaches, opponents, and others—who helped her out both as a tennis player and as a person. She keeps reminding the reader that she wasn't always easy to deal with. Her competitive nature sometimes got her into trouble, and even those who aided her most sometimes disapproved of her actions. But time and again, when she needed advice or encouragement—or even a place to live—someone was there.

Not all the help that athletes receive is given unselfishly. A coach may use a promising player to become famous himself. Some in the sports world may offer help so that they can gain control over a young and impressionable star. But Althea Gibson's story reminds us that there are many truly generous people in sport, and that an athlete may accept their help and still maintain a fine sense of independence.

The following account begins with Althea's introduction to tennis when she was 14.

AN AMAZINGLY GENEROUS THING

The 143rd Street block my mother and father lived on was a Police Athletic League play street, which means that the policemen put up wooden barricades at the ends of the street during the daytime and closed it to traffic so we could use it for a playground. One of the big games on the street was paddle tennis, and I was the champion of the block. In fact, I even won some medals representing 143rd Street in competition with other Harlem play streets. I still have them, too. I guess I've kept every medal or trophy I ever won anywhere.

Paddle tennis is played on a court marked off much like a tennis court, only about half the size. You use a wooden racket instead of a gut racket, and you can play with either a sponge rubber ball or a regular tennis ball. It's a lot different from real tennis, and yet it's a lot like it, too. There was a musician fellow, Buddy Walker, who was later known as "Harlem's Society Orchestra Leader," but who in those days didn't get much work in the summer months and filled in by working for the city as a play leader. He was watching me play paddle tennis one day when he suddenly got the idea that I might be able to play regular tennis just as well if I got the chance. So, out of the kindness of his heart, he bought me a couple of second-hand tennis rackets for five dollars apiece and started me out hitting balls against the wall on the handball courts at Morris Park. Buddy got very excited about how well I hit the ball, and he started telling me all about how much I would like the game and how it would be a good thing for me to become interested in it because I would meet a better class of people and have a chance to make something out of myself. He took me up to his apartment to meet his wife, Trini, and their daughter, Fern, and we all talked about it.

The next thing that happened was that Buddy took me to the Harlem River Tennis Courts at 150th Street and Seventh Avenue and had me play a couple of sets with one of his friends. He always has insisted that the way I played that day was phenomenal for a young girl with no experience, and I remember that a lot of the other players on the courts stopped their games to watch me. It was very exciting; it was a competitive sport and I am a competitive sort of person. When one of the men who saw me play that first time, a Negro schoolteacher, Juan Serrell, suggested to Buddy that he would like to try to work out some way for me to play at the Cosmopolitan Tennis Club, which he belonged to, I was more than willing. The Cosmopolitan is gone now, but in those days it was *the* ritzy tennis club in Harlem. All the Sugar Hill society people belonged to it.

Mr. Serrell's idea was to introduce me to the members of the Cosmopolitan and have me play a few sets with the club's one-armed professional, Fred Johnson, so that everybody could see what I could do. If I looked good enough, maybe some of them would be willing to chip in to pay for a junior membership for me and to underwrite the cost of my taking lessons from Mr. Johnson. Lucky for me, that's the way it worked out. I got a regular schedule of lessons from Mr. Johnson, and I began to learn something about the game of tennis. I already knew *how* to hit the ball but I didn't know *why*. He taught me some footwork and some court strategy, and along with that he also tried to help me improve my personal ways. He didn't like my arrogant attitude and he tried to show me why I should change. I don't think he got too far in that department; my mind was set pretty strong. I was willing to do what he said about tennis, but I figured what I did away from the courts was none of his business. I wasn't exactly ready to start studying how to be a fine lady.

I suppose if Fred Johnson or the club members who were paying for my tennis had known the whole truth about the way I was living I wouldn't have lasted long. The Cosmopolitan members were the highest class of Harlem people and they had rigid ideas about what was socially acceptable behavior. I'm ashamed to say I was still living pretty wild. I was supposed to be looking for a job, but I didn't look very hard because I was too busy playing tennis in the daytime and having fun at night. The hardest work I did, aside from practicing tennis, was to report to the Welfare ladies once a week, tell them how I was getting along, and pick up my allowance. Then I would celebrate by spending the whole day in the movies and filling myself up with a lot of cheap food. But I guess it would have been too much to expect me to change completely right away. Actually, I realize now that every day I played tennis and got more interested in the game, I was changing a little bit. I just wasn't aware of it.

One of the people who did a lot for me in those early days at the Cosmopolitan was Mrs. Rhoda Smith. She has been important to me ever since. Rhoda is a well-off society woman who had lost her own daughter about ten years before I met her, and she practically adopted me. She bought me my first tennis costume and did everything she could to give me a boost. I didn't always appreciate it, either, and I guess Rhoda was well aware of it. Years later she told a reporter: "I was the first woman Althea ever played tennis with, and she resented it because I was always trying to improve her ways. I kept saying, 'Don't do this,' and 'Don't do that,' and sooner or later she would holler, 'Mrs. Smith, you're always pickin' on me.' I guess I was, too, but I had to. When a loose ball rolled onto her court, she would simply bat it out of the way in any direction at all instead of politely sending it back to the player it belonged to, as is done in tennis. But Althea had played in the street all her life and she just didn't know any better."

I began taking lessons from Fred Johnson in the summer of 1941, but it wasn't until a year later that he entered me in my first tournament. The American Tennis Association, which is almost all Negro, was putting on a New York State Open Championship at the Cosmopolitan Club, and Fred put me in the girls' singles. It was the first tournament I had ever played in, and I won it. I was a little surprised about winning, but not much. By this time I was accustomed to winning games. I think what mostly made me feel good was that the girl I beat in the finals, Nina Irwin, was a white girl. I can't deny that that made the victory all the sweeter to me. It proved to my own satisfaction that I was not only as good as she was, I was better.

Later in the same year—the summer of 1942—the club took up a collection to send me to the A.T.A. national girls' championship at Lincoln University in Pennsylvania. That was my first national tournament, and I lost in the finals. The girl who beat me was Nana Davis, whose name is now

Nana Davis Vaughan, and I think it's interesting to read what Nana said about that match fifteen years later, after I won at Wimbledon:

"Althea was a very crude creature. She had the idea she was better than anybody. I can remember her saying, 'Who's this Nana Davis? Let me at her.' And after I beat her, she headed straight for the grandstand without bothering to shake hands. Some kid had been laughing at her and she was going to throw him out."

There wasn't any A.T.A. national championship tournament in 1943 because of the war and the restrictions on travel, but I won the girls' singles in both 1944 and 1945, and then, when I turned eighteen, my life began to change. For one thing, the social workers I had been reporting to no longer had charge of me. I wasn't a minor any more. Of course, I no longer was in line for the allowance I had been getting, either, but that didn't seem so important stacked up against the fact that I was able to run my own life at last. I had made friends with a girl named Gloria Nightingale, and I went to live with her in her family's apartment. I got a job as a waitress and I paid rent to Gloria's grandmother.

Gloria and I had a lot of fun together. During the winter of 1945–46, we played on the same basketball team—it was called The Mysterious Five—and we used to play as many as four or five games a week against different industrial teams. Whenever we weren't playing basketball we went bowling. Sometimes, even though it meant that we wouldn't get home until three or four in the morning, we would go bowling after we had finished a basketball game. Gloria was like me; all she cared about was playing games and having a good time. I still consider those years the liveliest of my whole life. We were really living. No responsibilities, no worries, just balling all the time.

It was through Gloria that I met Edna Mae and Sugar Ray Robinson [shortly before Sugar Ray became the world-champion boxer]. Gloria had known Edna Mae for a long time, and one night when we were out bowling we saw Ray in the place and she introduced me to him. To show you how cocky I was, I got on him right away. "So you're Sugar Ray Robinson?" I said. "Well, I can beat you bowling right now!" I think he took a liking to me right away. Anyway, from that night on, I used to go up to his place every chance I got. Whenever I could I would sleep there. Ray and Edna were real good friends; I felt that they liked me, and I was crazy about them.

Both Edna and Ray were kind to me in lots of ways. They seemed to understand that I needed a whole lot of help. I used to love to be with them. They had such nice things. Sometimes they would even let me practice driving one of their fancy cars, even though I didn't have a license. I think it gave Ray a kick to see how much fun I got out of it.

Ray had a set of drums that he liked to play and I always had an inkling for music myself. My favorite instrument was the saxophone. I just loved the sound of it. One day I asked

Edna if she thought Ray would buy me one, and she said the only way to find out was to ask him. So I did, and he told me that as long as I was really serious about it and not just fooling around, if I went to a music store or a hockshop and found one, he would pay for it. I've never forgotten it, and, for that matter, I still have the sax, although I haven't tried to play it in a long time.

Being eighteen, I was able to play in the A.T.A. national women's singles in 1946; I was out of the girls' class. I got to the finals and lost to Roumania Peters, a Tuskegee Institute teacher who was an experienced player; she had won the title in 1944. It was my inexperience that lost the match for me. Roumania was an old hand at tournament play and she pulled all the tricks in the trade on me. I wasn't ready for it. But I didn't feel too bad. There was no disgrace connected with losing in the finals.

I had played well enough, anyway, to attract the attention of two tennis-playing doctors, Dr. Hubert A. Eaton of Wilmington, North Carolina, and Dr. Robert W. Johnson of Lynchburg, Virginia, who were getting ready to change my whole life. They thought I was a good enough prospect to warrant special handling. I've often wondered if, even then, at that early stage of the game, they were thinking in terms of me someday playing at Forest Hills or Wimbledon. Whether they were or weren't, they certainly were looking to the future. It was their idea that what I ought to do first was go to college, where I could get an education and improve my tennis at the same time. "There are plenty of scholarships available for young people like you," Dr. Eaton told me. "It wouldn't be hard at all to get you fixed up at some place like Tuskegee."

"That would be great," I told him, "except I never even been to high school."

That stopped them for a while, but the two doctors talked it over with some of the other A.T.A. people and decided that I was too good a tennis prospect to let go to waste. The plan they finally came up with was for me to leave New York City and go to Wilmington to live with Dr. Eaton during the school year, go to high school there, and practice with him on his private backyard tennis court. In the summer I would live with Dr. Johnson in Lynchburg and I would travel with him in his car to play the tournament circuit. Each doctor would take me into his family as his own child and take care of whatever expenses came up during the part of the year I was with him. It was an amazingly generous thing for them to want to do, and I know I can never repay them for what they did for me.

Not that it was an easy decision for me to make. I was a city kid and I liked city ways. How did I know what it would be like for me in a small town, especially in the South? I'd heard enough stories to worry me. Up North, the law may not exactly be on your side, but at least it isn't always against you just because of the color of your skin. I would have to go into this strange country, where, according to what I'd heard, terrible things were done to Negroes just because they were Negroes, and nobody was ever punished for them. I wasn't at all sure going into something like that was a good idea. Harlem wasn't heaven but at least I knew I could take care of myself there.

I might have turned down the whole thing if Edna and Sugar Ray hadn't insisted that I should go. "You'll never amount to anything just bangin' around from one job to another like you been doin'," Ray told me. "No matter what you want to do, tennis or music or what, you'll be better at it if you get some education." In the end I decided he was right, and I wrote Dr. Eaton and told him I was coming. That was in August, 1946. He wrote me back and said I should get there by the first week in September. It didn't even leave me time to change my mind.

I went back to my mother and father's apartment to pack for the trip south. I used two suitcases; all my tennis clothes went into one and all the rest of my things into the other. Both of them were made of cardboard and they surely would have fallen apart if I hadn't tightened a spare belt around each one of them. I splurged on a taxicab to carry me down to Pennsylvania Station, and I must have been a sight to behold when I walked into the waiting room with a suitcase in each hand and Sugar Ray's saxophone hanging from a strap around my neck. I was so nervous about the whole thing, it was a miracle I didn't just check the bags and the sax, turn in the ticket Dr. Eaton had sent me, and go back to Harlem to see the matinee show at the Apollo. The ticket Dr. Eaton had bought for me was a coach fare, so I sat up all night on the trip from New York to Wilmington. For food, I bought peanut butter crackers, sandwiches and milk from the candy butcher who walked back and forth through the train. Every time I needed a dollar I reached for the little bankroll I had secured to the inside of my blouse with a great big safety pin. Fortunately, nobody sat next to me, so I was able to stretch out on the seat during the night and get a little sleep. Mostly, though, instead of sleeping, I just thought about what I was getting into. I thought about how lucky I was to be asked to live in a good home with people like the Eatons. I knew enough about the doctor to know that he was pretty well off financially and didn't lack for anything he wanted. I hoped I would do everything right, so they wouldn't be sorry they had started the whole thing. I made up my mind that I would adjust myself to whatever came along. But that didn't stop me from worrying about how it would be, about whether I would like it living in with the family, whether they would give me any money to spend on myself, would the movie houses refuse to let me in because I was colored, would I have to get off the sidewalk if a white person came along, and all kinds of things like that. By the time the conductor came through the car and called out, "The next station stop is Wilmington," I was as nervous as a cat. But when I got off, and saw this neatly dressed chauffeur coming up to me, and heard him ask if I was Althea Gibson, I began to feel better. Then, when I leaned back against the cushions in the back seat of Dr. Eaton's big car, and thought, ain't this a blip, he sure has nice things, this shouldn't be too hard to take. I felt pretty good.

I must have given Mrs. Eaton a turn when I got out of the car and walked through the kitchen door. I was wearing a tired old skirt that I had picked out because I figured it wouldn't matter if it got beat up on the train ride. I hated to wear anything except slacks, anyway, so I probably looked every bit as uncomfortable as I felt. I'd never owned a real dress since I'd been a little girl; a sweater and skirt combination was as far as I was willing to go in the direction of looking feminine. But Mrs. Eaton didn't bat an eye. I'd never met her before but she hugged me and kissed me as though I were her favorite niece. She was busy getting lunch ready, but she took time out to introduce me to the Eaton children and the maid and to show me to my room. Then she asked me if I was hungry, and when I said yes, I hadn't eaten any breakfast, she invited me to help myself to whatever I saw in the icebox that looked good to me. I fixed a couple of eggs and some bacon, cleaned up after, then looked all around the house and admired how nice it was. It was a far cry from what I'd been used to. Everything was as clean and as fresh as it could be. I can still remember running my fingers across the clean, starched white sheets on my bed and thinking how nice it would be to get right into it.

I was still in my room, putting away my things, when Dr. Eaton came home from his office, a little after three o'clock. He stood at the foot of the stairs and called up to me: "Althea! Althea!" I hurried out into the hall and said hello to him and said how beautiful my room was and how glad I was to be there, and he said, "You feel like hitting any, or are you too tired?" I said, "Oh, no, I feel fine. I'll be ready in a minute." And in just a few minutes I was out with the doctor on his handsome *en tout cas* court, trying to get a service ace past him, and my home life with the Eatons had officially begun.

The first big problem that had to be solved was where I would fit into the school. I didn't really have enough legitimate credits to get into the seventh grade, much less the second year of high school, which was what I hoped to talk my way into. But they gave me an aptitude test, and when they finished grading it they said they would assign me to the sophomore class and give me a chance to stick there if I could. That meant I would be able to earn my diploma in three years, and I was determined to do it. I buckled down to my schoolwork like nobody's business. I don't mean I was an angel. I still ducked off to the poolroom every chance I got, to relax a little, but I really hit those books.

Gradually, living in Dr. Eaton's house as one of the

family, I learned how to obey rules and get along with people. It was the first real family life I had ever known. Nobody stayed out all night in that house, or decided to eat lunch in a dog wagon downtown instead of coming home for lunch with the family. And the rules that applied to the Eatons' own children applied to me, too. I even got an allowance every week, the same as they did, so I could see that the good came with the bad. Not that there was anything bad about it, it was just that I wasn't used to living according to somebody else's plan. I'd been on my own for so long that I chafed under the discipline. Sometimes, naturally, I felt like rebelling, like doing what I wanted to do for a change. It just wasn't in me to be that good all the time. But, thank God, I never did anything really bad.

I worked hard on both my schoolwork and my tennis. I think the doctor was proud of what I did with both. I'm sure he was pleased with my tennis. He loved to see me beat the men he matched me against. His court was a gathering place for all the Negro tennis players of the district, as it had to be, because there wasn't any place else for them to play. There were a number of public courts in Wilmington, but no Negro could play on them. I'm glad to say there were quite a few fine white players who came to Dr. Eaton's to play with the good Negro players, and I often heard some of them criticize the stupidity of the segregation laws that kept them from playing together on the public courts.

The other big problem I had in Wilmington was the girls

in school. Most of them didn't like me at all. I'm not sure if maybe it wouldn't be more accurate to say they didn't understand me, but either way you put it, we didn't get along. I wasn't much for dressing up, even though Mrs. Eaton had bought me a few nice dresses and had had my hair curled and showed me how to put on lipstick. I still wore slacks and a T-shirt every chance I got, and because I loved to play basketball and baseball and football with the boys, all the girls thought I was the worst tomboy they'd ever seen. I was the star of the girls' basketball team, and later on they elected me the captain of it, but that wasn't enough athletic action to keep me happy, so I used to go out to the field during football and baseball practice and play with the varsity boys. It used to hurt me real bad to hear the girls talking about me when they saw me doing that. "Look at her throwin' that ball just like a man," they would say, and they looked at me like I was a freak. I hated them for it. I felt as though they ought to see that I didn't do the things they did because I didn't know how to, and that I showed off on the football field because throwing passes better than the varsity quarterback was a way for me to express myself, to show that there was something I was good at.

It seemed sometimes as though nobody could understand me. I've always liked to sing, and I went out for the school choir, figuring that that was one place where I ought to be able to fit in easily. But the instructor couldn't make up his mind what to do with me. First he put me in the alto section, but when he struck a chord and we began to sing in chorus, my voice sounded like a boy's in the middle of all the girls, and it ruined the whole thing. So the instructor said, "Well, let's try you in with the tenor boys. Maybe that'll work better." It did, as far as my singing was concerned, but the girls giggled so much about it that I got tired of it and quit.

At least I had my saxophone. I stayed in the marching band, and in the small jazz combo, as long as I was in school. There was no school tennis team, so I had to be satisfied with the tennis I played at Dr. Eaton's.

Then, during the vacation months, I went to Lynchburg and spent the summer playing with Dr. Johnson. I really worked there. I practiced with a Tom Stowe Stroke Developer, a robot machine that fired tennis balls across the net at me in a steady stream, and with every player who was willing to get out on the court and take me on. I played in nine tournaments that first summer, 1947, and won the singles championship in every one. Dr. Johnson and I won eight mixed doubles tournaments. One of the singles titles I won was the biggest that was open to me, the A.T.A. national women's singles, which I took by beating Nana Davis, 6-3, 6-0. It was the first of ten straight years that I won it. For whatever it was worth, I was the best woman player in Negro tennis.

I was lucky to have men like my two doctors looking out for me. Not only because they were doing so much for me in a material way, but because they were such high-type men. They were quite different, the two doctors, and yet they were very much alike. Dr. Eaton was tall, about six feet, and slim; Dr. Johnson was short and husky. Dr. Eaton, who was a graduate of the University of Michigan, was a quiet kind of man who liked tennis, golf and photography; Dr. Johnson, whose nickname was Whirlwind, was an active sportsman and a famous football player at Lincoln University when he was younger. Both of them were physician-surgeons with private clinics of their own, which is a common thing in Southern towns where Negro patients have to have a little clinic or hospital of their own because most of the time they aren't allowed in the white hospitals. And, last but not least, both of the doctors were ardent poker players.

As far as I'm concerned, one of the best hands of poker they ever played was dealing me into the big leagues of tennis. The first I heard about it was when Dr. Eaton sat down next to me at the A.T.A. championships in the summer of 1949 and said, very casually, "Althea, how would you like to play at Forest Hills?"

All I said was, "Huh! Who you kidding?" He knew I would give my right arm to play against the white girls, and he knew that I knew he knew it. I had talked about it often enough, although never as a genuine possibility, just as something that rankled me and ate at me.

"Well," he said, grinning a little like a cat who knows where the bottle of cream is, "I'm not saying for sure you're going to, but I'll say this much. It could happen. People are working on it."

"I'm ready," I told him. "I'm ready any time they are."

My first break came when the A.T.A. was notified that if I sent in an entry form for the Eastern Indoor Championships, to be played right in my old backyard in the armory at 143rd Street and Fifth Avenue in New York, I would be accepted. It was an especially good break for me because I was familiar with the surroundings and not likely to feel particularly strange. I did all right in the tournament. I played pretty well before Betty Rosenquest put me out in the quarter-finals, 8-6, 6-0, and I was reasonably satisfied. At least I hadn't been disgraced.

I felt even better when I was asked, right after my last match, if I would like to stay over in New York for another week and play in the National Indoor Championships. Once again, I lasted until the quarter-finals. I beat Ann Drye, 6-0, 6-1, in the first round, and Sylvia Knowles, 6-4, 3-6, 6-1, in the second. Then Nancy Chaffee got hold of me and put me out of the tournament. But I was glad I had lasted until the round of eight. I had been there, I had been invited to play with the white girls in one of the important tournaments, and I felt good about it. The world didn't have to reform overnight; I was willing to give it a few days.

Somewhat to my own surprise, because I'd had so little to do with books before I went to Wilmington, I finished up my high school course in three years, just as I had hoped I might be able to, and was graduated, in June, 1949, tenth in my class if you please. I was happy about it. I was twenty-one years old and I felt it was time I set out on my own. Partly I was ready to break loose and have a little fun, but partly I was dead serious about making something out of my life.

I remember a thing that happened around graduation time. All the girls in the senior class were ordering their class rings, and I wanted one badly. But I hated to ask Dr. Eaton for the money; they cost fifteen dollars, and it didn't seem fair to ask a man who had put out so much money for me already to buy something I didn't really need. So I sat down and wrote a few letters to people back in New York who I thought might be willing to help me, and I asked them if they could send me something toward the cost of the ring. The only one I ever heard from was Sugar Ray Robinson, and he sent me the whole fifteen dollars.

My last month in Wilmington I wrote letters to a number of Negro colleges, asking what chance I might have of getting a scholarship. As the two-time winner of the national Negro women's tennis championship, I had a pretty good claim. One of the schools that encouraged me was Florida A. and M., at Tallahassee. In fact, they did more than encourage me. Even before I got my high school diploma they wrote and said I was welcome to a scholarship

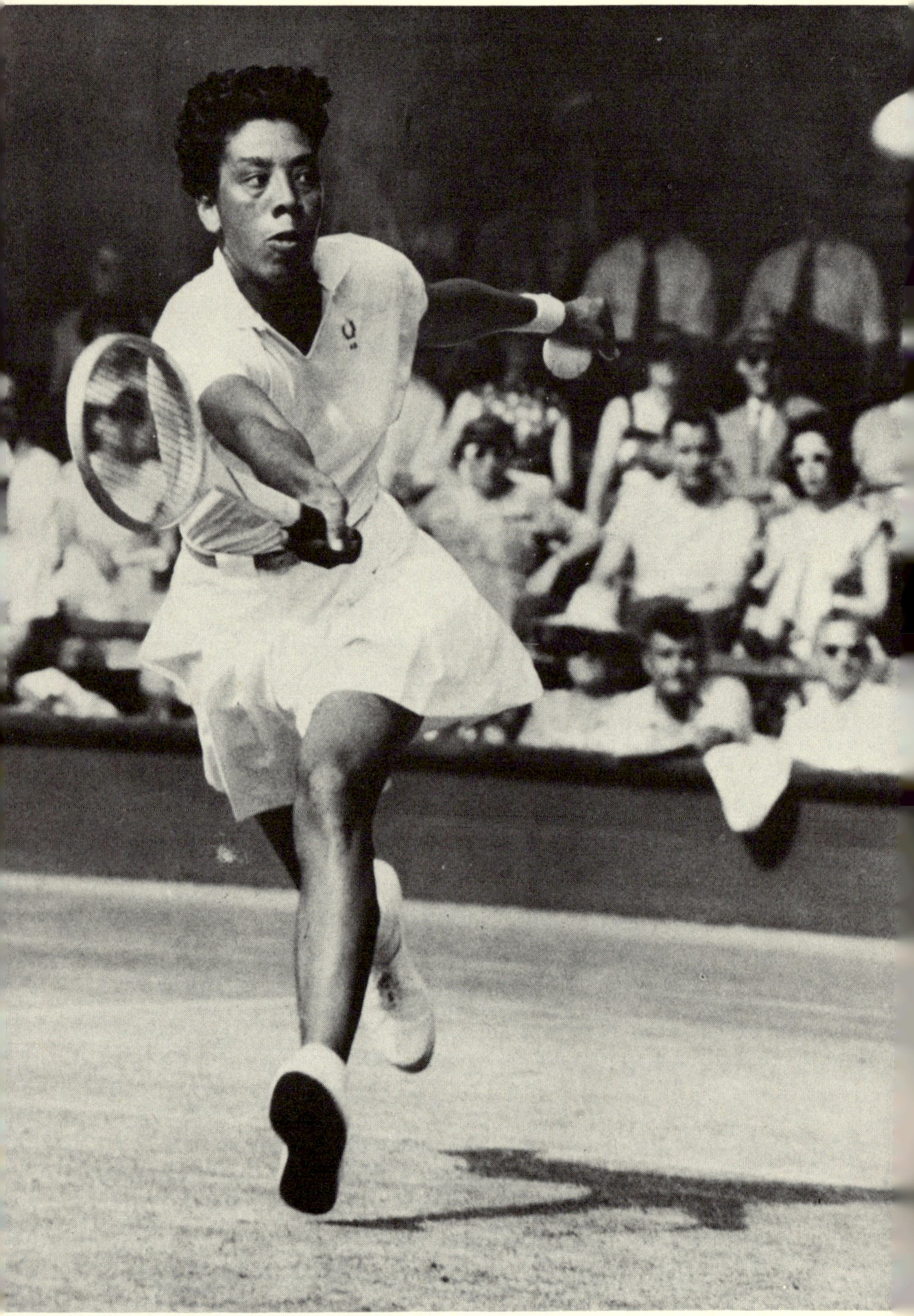

at A. and M., and that I should come down as soon as I got out of high school and spend the summer playing tennis down there.

I had my bags packed two days after graduation, and I was gone. I'm afraid the Eatons were a little bit hurt about the speed with which I left, but I couldn't help being eager to get started on my own. Nobody could have been more grateful than I was to both the doctors for everything they had done for me in those three years, but it was good to feel a little bit independent again. It's a feeling I've always been partial to.

■By the time Althea graduated from Florida A. and M. in 1953, she had played in the Nationals at Forest Hills, New York, and in other major American tournaments. From 1951 on she ranked among the top 20 women players in the world, but she always seemed to miss winning the big tournaments. Since she was an amateur, she sometimes had trouble making ends meet financially, and she seriously considered giving up the sport.

Finally in 1957 Althea played to the top of her capabilities and won the women's singles at Wimbledon, England, the most prestigious tournament in the world. At 30, after 16 years of play, she was recognized as the world's finest.

Her rise in tennis, breaking the color line for the first time

---

Althea Gibson playing at Wimbledon, England, in 1957— the year she won the women's singles.

and eventually becoming a world champion, was an inspiration to many, especially to black athletes and to women. Althea could claim much of the credit for herself. Few in her position would have had the tenacity to master a game dominated by the white and the rich and then play ten seasons for the championship. But some of the credit also belongs to those generous people—most of them black like Althea—who helped her into the world of tennis.

Ted Green
I CAN USE MY LEFT!

■The fear of injury haunts every athlete. In any sport a torn ligament, a broken ankle, or a sore arm may shorten an already brief athletic career. Injuries may come at any time, suddenly changing the course of the athlete's life and perhaps nipping his career in the bud.

If the injury heals, the athlete still faces a long road back. If he has been laid up for weeks or months, it will take him more weeks or months to get back into condition and to regain his timing and coordination. Then too there are psychological scars. Can the athlete forget the weakened knee or injured shoulder? Or will he continue to favor it instinctively long after it has healed? And will he have the nerve to risk injury again when he returns to competition?

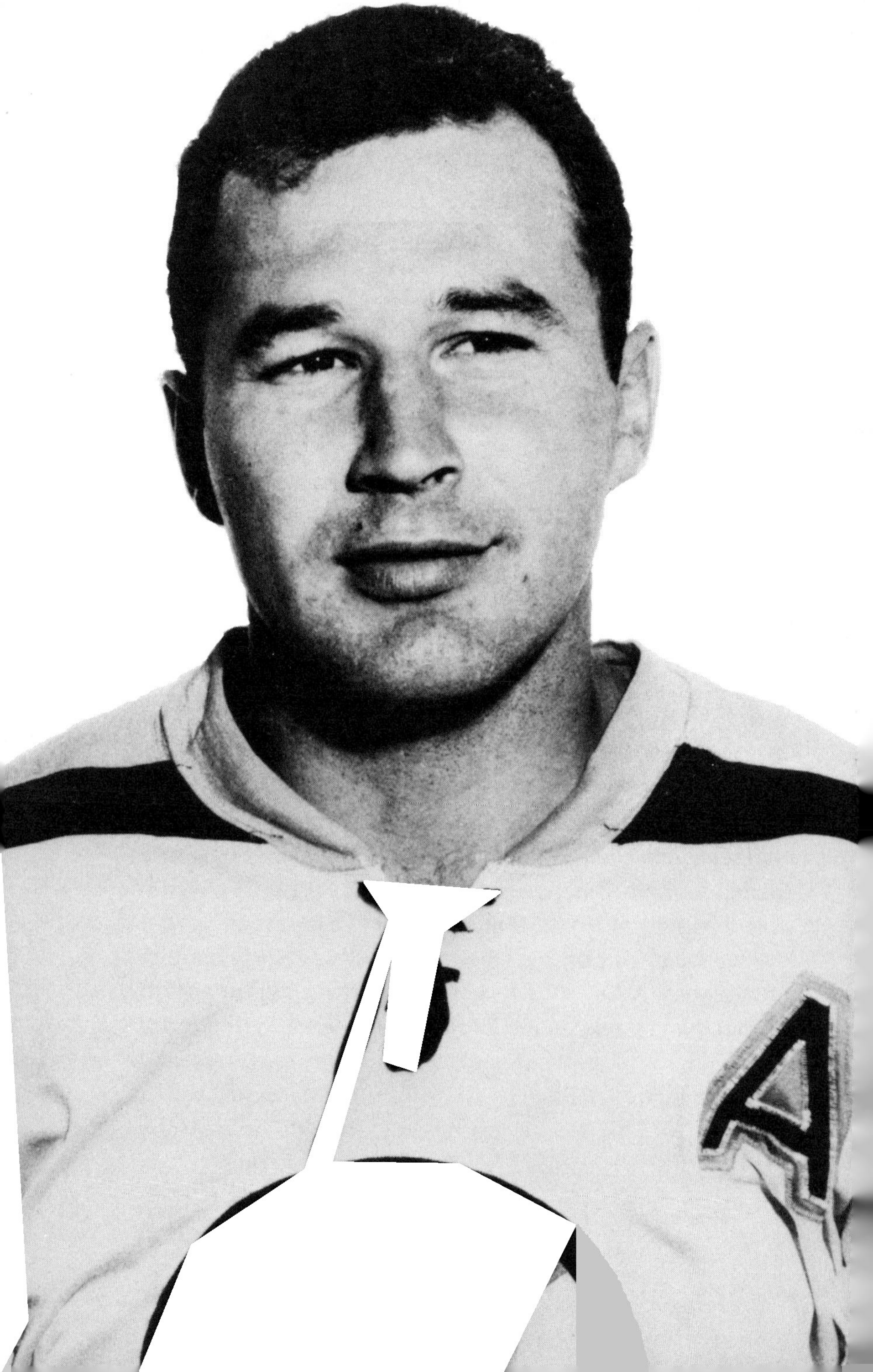

Ted Green, a defenseman for the Boston Bruins hockey team, was injured in an exhibition game in September of 1969. Another player hit him over the head with a hockey stick, fracturing his skull and causing brain damage. Green's left side was partially paralyzed for weeks and he had trouble speaking and writing. It seemed unlikely that he would ever play again.

But Green was determined to return to hockey. A year later he arrived at the Bruin training camp ready to relearn the game. His teammates, his wife, his fans, and others were eager to help him any way they could. But Green found that coming back was essentially a lonely, personal struggle.

Green was 30 years old when his injury occurred—at the height of his career. When he returned, he was back where he started, breaking in all over again almost like a rookie. He had to regain all of his physical skills and, even more difficult, overcome his own loss of confidence. He had to prove—to himself as well as to others—that he was good enough to play the game.

This account, an excerpt from Green's book *High Stick* (written with Al Hirshberg), begins early in the 1970–71 hockey season, fifteen months after Green was hurt.

Ted Green in 1968 with the Boston Bruins.

I CAN USE MY LEFT!

December 2, 1970. As I skated out to my right defense position for the Boston Bruins in the packed Chicago Stadium, I was thinking, *I wonder if this game will be better? I can't be sure.* Here we are, already halfway through the season, and I still don't want to be here. I don't like the nervous feeling I get when I go on the ice. I don't like thinking the way I'm thinking, or the way my hands sweat and my knees shake. I don't like not being able to do the job as I want to do it. My doctors and teammates tell me to forget these things—just think about playing hockey. It's so easy for them to say, so hard for me to do. I can't forget that easily—the nightmare is always there and I can't stop it.

I looked over at my defense partner, Don Awrey. We had just gone out to relieve Dallas Smith and Bobby Orr, a tough act to follow. Who can do the things Orr can do? Who can stop marveling at the way this kid makes all the right moves at the right times in the right places? I couldn't even have done them before Wayne Maki of the St. Louis Blues nearly killed me in September 1969. And now—

Now? So many nows—every game another now. Every game a little bit of extra hell. A question mark. A miracle. I could imagine what everyone in those big crowds that followed us around the circuit and packed the Boston

Garden when we played at home was thinking: *What will he do right? How much will he do wrong? He can't be the Terrible Teddy Green we remember. He can't do the things he used to do. They say he makes mistakes he never made before. They say he no longer has any inclination to fight. He wears a helmet. Whoever thought Terrible Teddy Green would need protection on his head or anywhere else? Or want it?*

Terrible Teddy Green. The tough guy of the National Hockey League. That was the reputation I had before Maki bashed in my skull with his stick during an exhibition game in Ottawa. I didn't like the name or the reputation. I played hockey hard, and sure I hit because it was my job to hit. In my younger days maybe I went out of my way to find a fight, but not later. Two, three years before Maki hit me, I had stopped being Terrible Teddy Green. I held my ground, I battled for puck control, I hit back when I got hit. But that was to protect my part of the ice, my goalie, my partner, and myself.

And when I had the puck, I bulled my way down the ice with it—passing and taking passes, fighting across the blue line and through opposing defensemen. And I was respected. *Leave Ted Green alone and you'll be OK. Just don't start anything with him, not unless you want to get into trouble.*

That's the way it had been, but not now. Physically, I was in as good shape as ever—maybe a little better. But as

162 ■ I CAN USE MY LEFT!

Coach Tom Johnson sent me on the ice that night in Chicago, I got that awful feeling of inadequacy which engulfed me all during the early season. I wasn't afraid—just unsure of myself. And in the NHL you can't be unsure of yourself. If there's one thing you need more than anything else, it's confidence. You're better than the other guy and you know it. Only I wasn't sure. That doubt was killing me, killing my game, making me wonder what I was doing out on the ice.

I wish I could express the feeling. Maybe one way is to describe what happened in a November game we'd lost to Oakland a few weeks before. I lost that game—I'm sure I did, and nobody can convince me otherwise. It was tied 1-1 in the third period when one of the Seals dumped the puck in on my side. Ordinarily this would have been no problem. I might have started up ice with it. Or, if a man were right on me and Awrey was free, I might have passed it across to Don. Or, if I got really tangled up with my opponent, I might have battled him to the boards to freeze the puck and force a faceoff.

I didn't do any of these things. In fact, I'm not sure what I did. All I know is that one minute I had control of the puck, and the next instant I didn't. One of the Seals' guys just swooped down, stole it right from under me, and with nobody in front of the net but our goalie, Eddie Johnston, slammed it home for a 2-1 win for them. Johnston didn't have a chance.

Maybe I was imagining things, but I could hear the crowd murmuring that night, too: *He lost the puck. . . . He never did it that way before. . . . Teddy Green hasn't got it anymore. . . . Give him "A" for effort, but he just isn't the hockey player he was. . . .*

Later, in the dressing room, the guys came over with a word or two of encouragement. My buddy, Eddie Johnston, telling me it wasn't my fault. Derek "Turk" Sanderson and Phil Esposito, whose lockers are near mine, saying everybody makes mistakes—Turk, in fact, calling hockey a game of mistakes, which I suppose it is. Bobby Orr coming over to tell me not to blame myself. Eddie Westfall, who broke into the Bruins with me, saying something to make me feel better. I don't think a single player didn't stop by as I sat staring, unseeing, into my locker.

And still later, long after I showered and dressed for the street, there was Pat, my wife, who never missed a home game, never let a chance go by to buck me up, never admitted to herself or anyone else that anything that went wrong was my fault, waiting at the door for me. I looked at her, and with tears in my eyes I just raised my hands in a gesture of frustration.

Neither of us said anything until we were in the car heading home. Then I muttered, "I lost it."

"You didn't lose it, Ted," Pat said emphatically. "No one man loses a game."

"I lost this one."

"You made a mistake. Everybody makes mistakes."

"They were all saying the same things in the locker room," I said. "But they knew—they all knew. And you know. If I had kept control of that puck, we wouldn't have lost the game. But it slipped away from me."

"Don't think about that, Ted. It's happened before and it will happen again."

"That's it, honey," I said. "It hasn't happened before—not for years, not since I was a kid. I never made mistakes like that."

"You're looking for miracles," she said. "You've made miracles already. Every doctor, coach, trainer—everyone who's helped—said you wouldn't even be on skates until January. You were on skates the day the training season opened, less than a year after you were hurt. And you've been playing in the fastest hockey league in the world since the season started."

"And I cost us a game."

As I stood out on the ice in Chicago, memories of that Oakland loss and of all those early games flashed through my mind. Despite my reputation, I hadn't been looking for fights even before I was hurt—I just never ran away from them. Now I was avoiding them, backtracking if one seemed to be coming my way. If I was lucky, I could divert a man into the corner, but I didn't fight him, didn't battle, didn't try to crash him into the boards, didn't swing at him, grab him, or do anything to get the puck away from him. I could almost hear the word getting around the league: *Go down Green's side. The poor guy can't do anything. He's helpless against a big rush. He doesn't get in the way anymore. He won't hit and he can't hurt.*

Even worse than that were those other words going through the league: *Don't go after Green. Don't try to hurt him. He's been hurt enough. He's making a game attempt to do the impossible. Don't hit him unless you have to—and then don't hit him hard. He's a good guy and he deserves every break.* Pity. Compassion. Sympathy. That was the most horrible thing. I didn't want that—I wanted to earn my way back, to have the respect of my opponents the way it was before I got hurt.

The brain damage had all been on the right side of my head, which controls nerves on the left side—and I'm left-handed. The doctor had assured me my left side was as strong as ever, the plastic coating over the hole in my head sturdier than the bone it had replaced. I didn't have to worry about it anymore. And yet I did. *Terrible Teddy Green worried? Why?* Perhaps "worry" is the wrong word. I didn't care about getting hit, nor did I turn my right side to catch a possible check and absorb the shock. It was more a loss of confidence and of timing than worry.

On that December night at the Chicago Stadium, I still wasn't myself. I had shown an occasional flash, but I hadn't got into a single fight, hadn't thrown a punch, hadn't bulled my way past anybody. I had made only a few good checks and sometimes an accurate pass—outside of my skating, my passing was really the first thing that came back—but I needed confidence, and I didn't have it yet.

I couldn't understand why. Before games, I had no trouble psyching myself up. I could psych myself just as well after Maki hurt me as before. The difference came when I skated out on the ice. All the psyching in the world couldn't keep me calm and confident, not in those early months of the 1970–71 season. I shook, I worried, I wondered. Sometimes I felt that way all evening. Other times I got over it after two or three turns on the ice. But I couldn't get rid of it altogether, and that worried me more than anything.

It was this feeling—and, I'm sure, only this feeling—that gave me a tendency to lose shots I should have blocked. This is one of a defenseman's prime jobs, and I wasn't doing it as often as I should. When I did do it, I felt good because then I knew I was functioning properly. But blocking shots shouldn't have made me so happy. In the old days, it was second nature. Now it had become the exception.

Funny, in all these early games, right up to the one in Chicago on December 2, the same thoughts flashed through my head. That was one of the problems. I was thinking too much. What made me an NHL star were things I did without thinking. The moves were natural, a part of me. I

After his injury, Teddy Green wore a helmet on the ice.

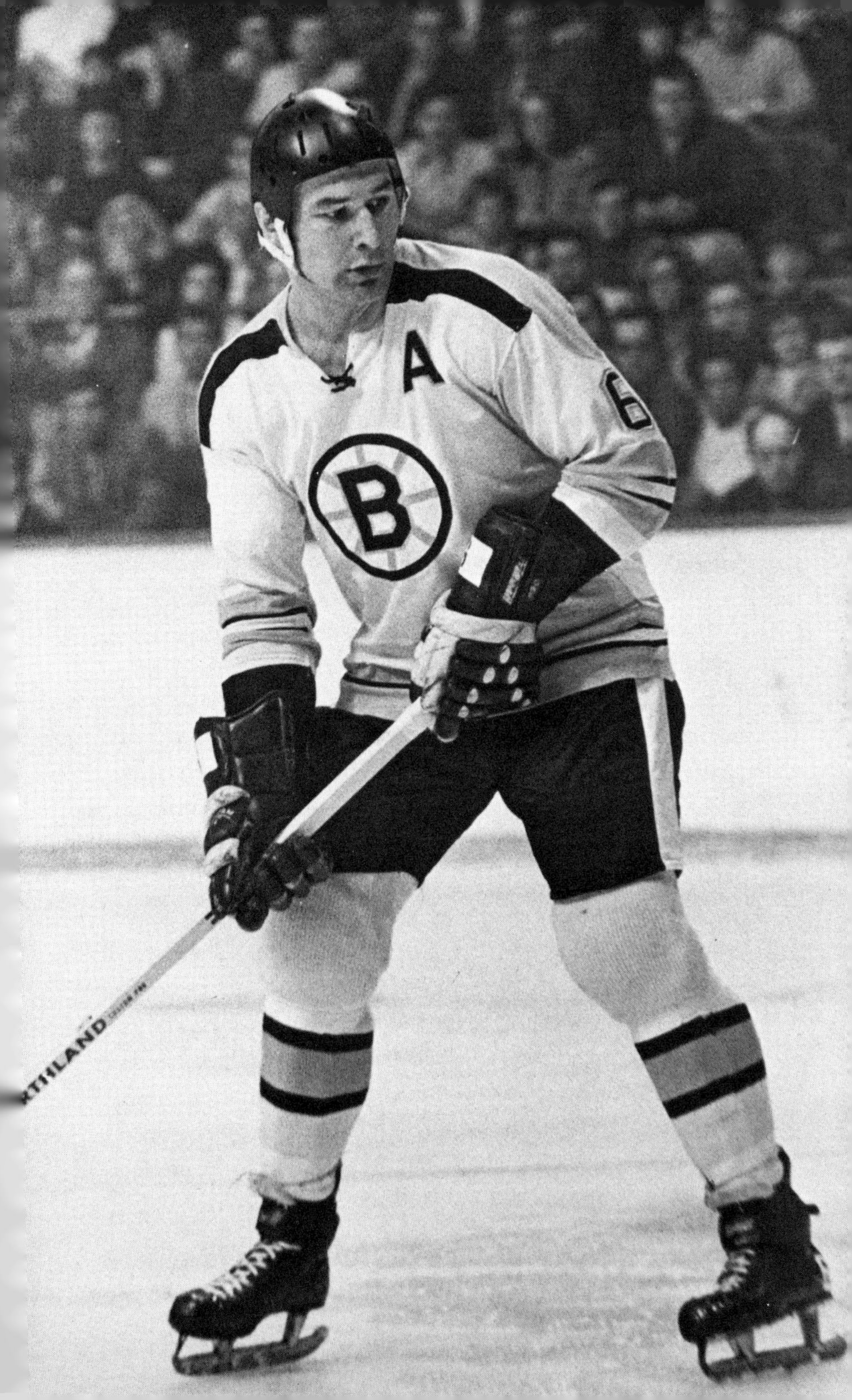
A
6
B

didn't have to think, *I'm going to hit this guy*—I just hit him. I didn't have to think, *I'm going to block the puck*—I just blocked it.

Now everything was mental. It was a problem I had to lick. If I didn't, it would lick me. After all I had gone through to get into shape to return to the NHL, I *couldn't* let overthinking get the better of me. Something had to happen to help me conquer it—or maybe, without conscious thought, I could make something happen.

For this reason the December 2 game in Chicago was so important. That was the night something in me opened up and let all the gremlins out. That was the night I became the old Teddy Green, the Teddy Green I had been, the Teddy Green I wanted to be again. I made mistakes in later games, and once in a while I still got the shakes, but on December 2, I turned the corner and started moving in the right direction. That was the night my confidence returned. I knew for sure I was going to make it, after all.

It was a rough game, with a lot of pushing and elbowing and scrambling—one of those games you know will blow sky-high sooner or later. About halfway through the second period, when Don Awrey got into a fight with one of the Black Hawk players, I skated over to give him a hand. I definitely wasn't looking for a fight—all I wanted to do was break up this one. As I approached the two guys battling near the boards on the left side of our defensive zone, Dan Maloney, a 20-year-old Chicago rookie who stands six feet and weighs about 200 pounds, grabbed Awrey from behind and started punching him. In the short time Maloney had been in the league, we'd learned he was a "sucker" puncher—somebody who makes a specialty of surprising an opponent by hitting him when he's not looking or is busy fighting somebody else, as Awrey was.

My original reason for going over to where Awrey was fighting was to help him, and maybe Maloney's reason for suckering him was to help a Chicago player. In any event, Maloney had already hit Awrey and was trying to hold him from behind when I got there. By then, all I wanted to do was get Maloney—get the kid off Awrey's back so Don could keep swinging, or at least protect himself. I dropped my stick and gloves and started hauling Maloney off Awrey. As I pinned his arms and pulled him away, Maloney said, "Let go, I'm not going to hit you."

Knowing his tendencies, I wasn't going to fall for that without being ready to protect myself—in fact, I didn't want to fight at all because I still wasn't sure of myself. But since he was now clear of Awrey, I let him go, and, sure enough, he tried to sucker me. I ducked, and his punch went over my shoulder and by my head. My helmet slipped down over my face, scratching my nose, and I blew up. While I yanked at the helmet, Maloney tried to sucker me again, and again he missed. By the time I was rid of that damn helmet, instinct took over and I could swing freely. I did it naturally—left-handed. I nailed him with four good lefts in a row, hitting him so hard that he started sliding down the side boards onto the ice. Somebody had to pull me off before I stopped swinging. The way I was hitting the kid, I'd have knocked him cold. As it was, I dazed him, and he had to go to the dressing room when most of us drew penalties.

I guess I wasn't even thinking as I picked up my gloves and stick and skated over to the penalty box. But I felt a sudden warmth, the comfort that comes when something very good happens.

I felt these things rather than thinking them. I was grinning, almost laughing, as I served my time in the penalty box. And I grinned still more after getting out when I went over to our bench, where the guys were yelling and laughing and throwing friendly punches at me.

Not until then did I realize the little finger on my left hand hurt like hell. This was curious, because one of the first effects of my skull fracture had been paralysis of my left side, including numbness in my hands and fingers. Actually, even that long after the injury, I couldn't write easily or clearly, and—as is still the case—I had no feeling in the tips of the fingers of my left hand. I looked down and saw the little finger was crooked. I tried to move it and almost yelled with pain.

Then I smiled—smiled like a crazy man. *God, I thought, I broke my finger throwing punches. Imagine, I belted him so hard I broke my finger—and on my left hand!* I studied my hand again. Except for the little finger, it was fine. I found Frosty Foristall, our assistant trainer, and eased over to him.

"My finger's sore," I said. "I've got to keep playing tonight, so fix it up."

"It looks broken," Frosty said.

"It probably is," I said. "Do something."

Frosty quickly made a little mold for a temporary splint, while I thought, *I can use my left—I can use my left—I can use my left.* The words rang in my mind as Frosty worked so fast I don't think I missed a turn on the ice. When Tom Johnson gave the word, I jumped the boards with Awrey, ready for anything.

I played the rest of the game with that broken finger, and not only did I not worry about what might happen, I played exceptionally well. Nothing much happened, really. The Hawks had learned something, too, and they left me alone. When the puck came into my zone, nobody came barreling hard after it the way everyone had before. Nobody wanted to tangle with me, or start a fight, or try to belt me around. *They're not afraid of hurting me anymore,* I thought. *They're afraid of my hurting them.*

We lost the game, which didn't make me happy, but my heart was singing when it was over. They could call me Terrible Teddy Green all they wanted to now. It was just an incident, but what an incident! It taught me to feel what everyone, including the doctors who checked me from time to time, had been telling me right along—my left side was strong, and I could expose it to anything I had ever exposed it to before, and it would hold up.

In the locker room later, Frosty and Dan Canney, our head trainer, made a removable metal splint, while guys came in and out, joking and patting my back and saying things like, "What the hell's a broken finger?" Despite the loss, they were happy for me. They knew I had found something I'd been looking for all year—myself, the old Teddy Green.

■Green successfully completed the season with the Bruins. Later he jumped to the New England Whalers of the new World Hockey Association where he was recognized as one of the best defensemen in the league. Was he as good as he had been before his injury? No one would ever know for sure. But Green had the satisfaction of coming back from an injury that would have caused most others to give up in despair.

Jackie Robinson
THE GUTS NOT TO FIGHT BACK

■Sporting events rarely have much influence in the larger world. But once in a while sport takes on added significance —it ceases to be merely a game and becomes a symbol of something greater. One such instance was the arrival of Jackie Robinson, a black man, in organized baseball.

In 1945, when our story begins, Jackie Robinson was 26 years old. He had been a great college athlete in football, baseball, and basketball at UCLA. Then he had served in the Army during World War II, gaining a reputation as a fighter for the rights of black soldiers. He had forced the Army to accept him and other blacks into Officer Candidate's School and had fought for the integration of the Post Exchange, the military base's general store.

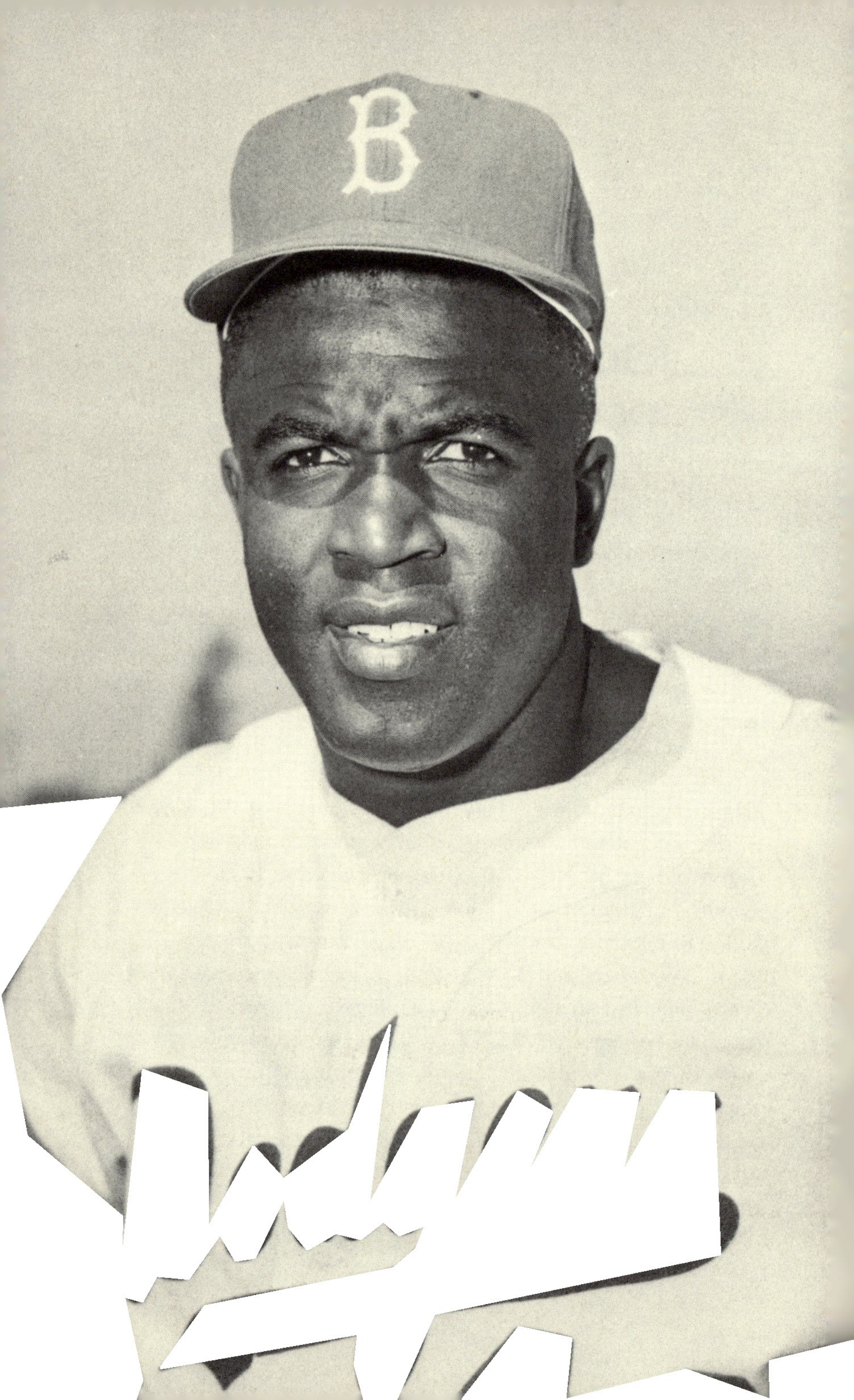

Now he was beginning a career in baseball. Would he ever play in the major leagues? He had no reason to think so. Organized baseball (the major leagues and their minor league affiliates) employed white players only. Robinson would have to be satisfied playing at a low salary in the Negro leagues—or so it seemed.

The segregation in baseball reflected the segregation in most areas of American life. In the South, laws required that blacks attend separate schools, stay in separate hotels, ride at the back of buses, even drink at separate water fountains. North and South, blacks were excluded by law or custom from living in white neighborhoods and from being considered for most well-paying jobs.

But at least in baseball, times were changing. One general manager, Branch Rickey of the major league Brooklyn Dodgers, was quietly making plans to introduce black players into organized baseball. His choice for the first black player was Jackie Robinson.

For a young athlete like Robinson, being first would be an uneviable job, full of stress and danger. Those who opposed the mixing of the races would cheer his every mistake, hoping that he would fail. And millions of black fans would be following his every move, considering his victories or defeats as their own. Any young athlete breaking into professional baseball would feel the pressure to succeed, but

---

Jackie Robinson, 1956, as he is best remembered by millions of baseball fans.

Jackie would have the extra pressure of leading a social revolution. And the hardest part of all was that Jackie would be asked to suppress his instinct to fight back until baseball learned to accept the mere presence of a black man.

The following excerpts (taken from *Wait Till Next Year*, which Carl Rowan wrote with Jackie) illustrate the personal courage and control that Robinson showed in his early months in white baseball. They begin with Rowan's famous account of Jackie's first meeting with Branch Rickey of the Dodgers. It was at this meeting that Robinson first learned of Rickey's hopes for him. Rickey made no secret of the difficulties that lay ahead.

THE GUTS NOT TO FIGHT BACK

"Tell me, Jackie, do you have any idea why I want to talk to you?"

"All I know is what Mr. Sukeforth [a Dodger scout] told me, and the rumors I've been hearing about you starting a new Negro league and a team called the Brown Dodgers."

"No, Jackie, that isn't really it. You were brought here to play for the Brooklyn organization—perhaps, as a start, for Montreal."

"Me? Me play with Montreal . . . ?"

"If you can make it. If you make the grade. We scouted

you for weeks, Jackie. We know what you can do on the baseball field. But this means more than being able to play baseball. I mean, have you got the guts?"

"I'll make it if I get the opportunity . . ." said Robinson.

"I want to be honest with you, Jackie. I want to level with you here today. I heard all the stories of racial resentment toward you. They told me out in Pasadena that you're a racial agitator. They told me at UCLA that in basketball you had trouble with coaches, players and officials. I just want to tell you that my thorough investigation convinced me that the criticisms are unjustified, that if you'd been white it would have been nothing. So I'm dismissing these rumors as not amounting to a hill of beans. But the thing I want to convince you of is that we can't fight our way through this. Jackie, we've got no army. There's virtually nobody on our side. No owners, no umpires, very few newspapermen. And I'm afraid that many fans may be hostile. We'll be in a tough position, Jackie. We can win only if we can convince the world that I'm doing this because you're a great ballplayer, a fine gentleman.

"Have you got the guts to play the game no matter what happens? That's what I want to know!" Rickey exclaimed.

"I think I can play the game, Mr. Rickey," said Robinson.

"All right. You're standing in the batter's box in a tense situation. I'm a notorious bean-baller. I wing a fast one at you that grazes your cap and sends you sprawling back on your butt. What do you do?"

178 ■ THE GUTS NOT TO FIGHT BACK

"It won't be the first time a pitcher threw one at me, Mr. Rickey," Robinson said matter-of-factly.

"All right. So I'm an opposing player, and we're in the heat of a crucial game. I slap the ball out into the field and I'm rounding first and I charge into second and we have a close play and I collide with you. As we untangle I lunge toward you"—Rickey lunged toward Robinson—"and I shout, 'Get out of my way, you dirty black son of a bitch!' What do you do?"

Robinson was silent. He looked at Rickey, and he licked his lips and swallowed. He knew the answer Rickey wanted. That he would grin and bear it. But before he could get the answer out, Rickey was unfolding another situation.

"You're playing shortstop and I come down from first, stealing, flying in with my spikes high, and I cut you in the leg. As the blood trickles down your shin I grin at you and say, 'Now how do you like that, nigger boy?' What do you do?"

Robinson was burning hot inside. His whole life had been an effort to convince the white people around him that no matter what had ever been said, the Negro was not a coward—not a coward against any odds. "Mr. Rickey," he said, "do you want a ballplayer who's afraid to fight back?"

Rickey shouted, "I want a ballplayer with guts enough not to fight back!

"Remember what I said, Jackie. This is one battle we can't *fight* our way through. Remember what I said, Jackie:

no army, no owners, no umpires, virtually nobody on our side. This is a battle in which you'll have to swallow an awful lot of pride and count on base hits and stolen bases to do the job. That's what'll do it, Jackie. Nothing else."

But Branch Rickey was not through. He posed as a hotel clerk telling Robinson that "no niggers can sleep here"; as a restaurant manager telling Robinson that he couldn't eat out front with the rest of the team, but that they would prepare sandwiches for him to eat in the bus, or fix him a meal in the kitchen; as an umpire calling Robinson out on a bum decision and then barking out angry words reflecting on the color of Robinson's face.

"Now we're in the World Series," Rickey continued. "We play for keeps, there, Jackie; we play it there to win, and almost everything under the sun goes. I want to win in the most desperate way, so I'm coming into second with my spikes flying. But you don't give ground. You're tricky. You feint, and as I hurl myself you ease out of the way and jam that ball hard into my ribs. As I lie there in the swirling dust, my rib aching, I hear that umpire crying, 'You're out,' and I jump up, and all I can see is that black face of yours shining in front of my eyes. So I yell, 'Don't hit me with a ball like that, you tarbaby son of a bitch.' So I haul off and I sock you right in the cheek." Rickey waved his massive fist in Robinson's face, missing it only by a whisper. Robinson's nose twitched and his lips moved a bit. But his head was steady.

"I get it, Mr. Rickey, I get it," the Negro said. "What you want me to say is that I've got another cheek."

Rickey smiled with satisfaction.

When their three-hour conference was over, Branch Rickey held no doubt that Jackie Robinson was the man he wanted. Robinson agreed to accept a bonus of $3,500 and a salary of $600 a month as part of what was, in effect, a contract to play baseball with the Montreal Royals in 1946.

■Before reporting for spring training, Robinson went home to California and was married to his college sweetheart Rachel (Rae) Isum. Then in February of 1946, Jackie and Rae prepared to fly to the Dodger training camp in Florida. Jackie's mother came to the airport to see the young couple off. As they were about to board the plane, Mrs. Robinson gave them a shoebox full of fried chicken and hard-boiled eggs. Jackie and Rae were embarrassed by the picnic lunch, but they took it along.

This would be the first time either Jackie or Rae had visited the Deep South. Rae tells about the trip—and about how it brought home to her and Jackie the obstacles they would face in the years to come.

We had reservations to Daytona Beach, with a change of planes at New Orleans. We reached New Orleans at about 7:00 A.M. and were supposed to leave at 11:00 A.M. When the eleven o'clock plane came, airline officials told us that we had been shifted to a twelve o'clock flight. Later they

Jackie Robinson ■ 181

told us that we would get out on a later plane. We asked if there was any place where we might rest while awaiting our flight and found that there was no place for a Negro to rest at the New Orleans airport. We asked about food and were told that there was a restaurant where we could purchase sandwiches, but we would have to bring them out to eat them. Jack almost exploded at this suggestion. The pride in both of us had rebelled, so under no circumstances would we accept food on this basis.

The airline agent suggested that we go to a hotel to relax until they called us. We went, remembering happily now that we still had that shoebox full of chicken and boiled eggs. We ate it with glee. It occurred to us for the first time that the stereotype about Negro "picnics" on trains probably grew out of just this kind of situation—Negroes packing a lunch because of knowledge that dining cars and restaurants would refuse them service.

I suppose there must have been a better hotel for Negroes in New Orleans, but neither Jack nor our driver knew of it. We entered this place and I was almost nauseated. It was a dirty, dreadful place, and they had plastic mattress covers! Lying on the bed was like trying to sleep on newspapers. We gave the airline our telephone number, and they told us we probably would leave in four hours, but that if there was any change they would telephone us. They didn't call, so we checked with them and were told to come to the airport. When we showed up we were told that there would be another delay, so we sat for several more hours. Finally, about 7:00 P.M., we were notified that we had seats to Daytona Beach.

We were being paged as the plane landed at Pensacola, Florida, however, and Jackie got off to see why. The stewardess said to me, "You'd better get off, too." I was puzzled. I watched closely as she asked another passenger, a Mexican, to get off.

I gathered up my things and went into the airport to find Jack in a heated argument with the manager. "What's the matter?" I said. Jack replied, "We've been taken off the plane. The manager said that they were expecting a storm and had to take three passengers off to load on more fuel."

"Take off passengers to put on fuel?" I said. "Why, I just saw two white passengers get on and take our seats on the plane."

"Well, er, uh, that's another reason. They forgot to leave enough empty seats available in New Orleans for passengers to board at Pensacola."

Jack protested vociferously, but I knew that this would be of little avail in Pensacola. That was one of the big differences, I soon discovered, between injustice in the Deep South and injustice in the North or on the West Coast. In the latter communities a Negro had some recourse, particularly where the law or public opinion was on his side and the side of decency; but here in Florida we realized that the law, public opinion and custom all weighed against us, so there was nothing for us to do but get off the plane. It seemed more than mere coincidence.

We were notified that another plane was coming through the next morning, but that the airline could guarantee us no space on it. Meanwhile Jack was due at spring training the morning after next and under the circumstances—his first visit to spring training, the entire sports world watching him and his conduct—he was anxious to be on time. We asked the airline agent what we should do and he said he would provide a limousine to take us into town and find us a place to stay for the night, and we would have to take a train or bus out in the morning, unless we wanted to gamble on another flight.

The limousine driver was sympathetic, talking at great length about what a shame he thought it was to put us in this position. He said, however, that he hadn't the faintest idea where to take two Negroes to spend the night in Pensacola.

"I'll take you by a white hotel and I can ask some of the colored bellboys if they know where you can spend the night," he said. A bellboy gave him the name and address of a Negro family which would rent us a room. The driver took us to this house, placed our luggage on the porch and drove away. We entered to find that this small frame house was almost overrun with children. The family was using the living room to sleep in, and it was obvious that there was no place for us. But the woman was extremely nice. She said she would make room for us somehow, but we could see there wasn't even room for our luggage.

We learned that a bus would soon leave for Jacksonville, so we decided to take it. When we boarded, only a handful of people were on the bus. They were white, and seated at the front. We were terribly tired and I walked eagerly to the last of the reclining seats near the rear, hoping I could sleep through the greater part of this trip to Jacksonville. Jackie fell asleep before I did. We had traveled only a few miles when, at one of the stops, the driver walked up to me and merely motioned with his hand toward the long seat at the rear. I wondered if it was arrogance or shame that kept him from telling us verbally that the Jim Crow laws of Florida, as he interpreted them, forbade us to sit in the reclining seats that were only one row from the rear of the bus. I woke Jack and we moved to the back seat.

For sixteen hours we bounced and jogged at the rear of this bus, and often I was almost nauseated by the engine fumes that wafted in through the open window. Now I understood why this was the space reserved for Negroes.

At daybreak Negro working men crowded on. The Jim Crow section got so jammed that we took turns standing and sitting, although there were several empty seats in the white section. I looked at my new going-away trousseau suit and the ermine coat that Jack had saved for years to buy me as a wedding gift, and I could see the stains from the overalls worn by men going to work in the fields and the rock quarries. I felt like weeping.

We ate nothing throughout this trip because we refused to ask for food from back doors and windows. I had never been so tired, hungry, miserable and upset in my life as when we finally reached Daytona Beach.

During that bus ride, when we were alternating between sitting and standing, or first one person would sit forward on the edge of the seat and another would sit far back so as to accommodate more people, I buried my head behind the seat in front of me and wept silently. I didn't want Jack to see me cry, but I was so unhappy; it's just that I had never seen him in that position before, unable to be a man and assert himself, unable to take care of me, having to obey quietly when that driver ordered us to the rear.

■From Daytona Beach, the Robinsons went on to the Dodger camp in the small town of Sanford, Florida. Now Jackie takes up the story, describing his arrival on the first day of practice. Clyde Sukeforth, the Dodger scout, was there to introduce Robinson and Johnny Wright, another black prospect, to the Dodger staff.

Before going into the clubhouse I glanced at the players out on that field—two hundred men, all of them eager for a place high in the Dodger organization, each of them representing my competition, and a great number of them from the South. They were hitting fungoes, huffing and puffing around the field, with sweat streaming from their faces, throwing balls to each other, keeping up a constant barrage of the chatter that seems to go with baseball, especially training sessions. As I made this momentary survey of the situation it seemed that every one of those men stopped suddenly in his tracks and that four hundred eyes were trained on Wright and me.

When we walked onto the field a group of reporters from northern newspapers began a barrage of questions.

"Jackie, you think you can get along with these white boys?"

"I've gotten along with white boys at UCLA, at Pasadena, in high school and in the Army. I don't know why these should be any different."

"What will you do if one of these pitchers throws at your head?"

"I'll duck like everyone else."

There was a ripple of laughter from the newspapermen.

"Do you think you can win the shortstop job from Stanley Breard?" Breard, I knew, was the most popular player on the Montreal team.

"I don't know whether I can win any job or not. I just mean to do the best I can."

"Do you have hopes of playing with Brooklyn some day?"

"Of course I do, just like all those other players out there."

"That means you're out after Pee Wee Reese's job, since

you're a shortstop."

"Now wait a minute—it doesn't mean I'm out after any individual's job. It just means that I'm going to do my darndest to make the team, then I'll play wherever I can best help the team. I'm just like all other players in that respect. Right now, though, I can't worry about Brooklyn. I haven't made the Montreal team yet."

Sukeforth shooed the newspapermen away and took us to meet Clay Hopper, the Montreal manager. I faced this introduction with a great deal of uneasiness, for I had read that Hopper was a Mississippi plantation owner, and I had heard from several friendly newspapermen that he had something less than the reputation of a great friend of the Negro.

"Clay, this is Robinson and Wright," said Sukeforth.

"Hello, Jackie," Hopper said. I was relieved to see him stick out his hand, for even in those days great numbers of southerners would under no circumstances shake hands with a Negro. After the introduction we made polite conversation about the kind of winter rest we had had and then, in a deep, soft southern drawl, Hopper told us that we were not to do too much that day—just throw the ball around awhile and hit a few.

Sukeforth then introduced me to two players with whom I was to throw. I tried to concentrate on the training exercises, but I was constantly interrupted by photographers—so much so that it was embarrassing. They wanted me to pose leaping to catch a ball, running the bases, sliding, throwing. It bothered me that I remained the center of attention, for I felt that my best chance for success would come if I could get at least some of these people to stop thinking of me as a Negro, to let me fade into the crowd where I then would stand out only because of such fielding and hitting as I might do.

■On the second evening of their stay in Sanford, Jackie and Rae received sudden orders to pack their bags and return to the main camp at Daytona Beach. They later discovered that threats of violence from the local townspeople had forced the Dodgers to move them. Jackie was upset, and in trying to make up for the trouble by playing extra hard on the field, he almost lost everything.

I went to practice the next day determined to show Manager Hopper that I really could play baseball. I was on the second team. Breard, the fine French Canadian, was first-team shortstop. In trying to impress Hopper, I raced all over the infield trying to make sensational stops, and I pegged the ball to first base as hard as I could, attempting to belie reports that I had a weak arm. Sukie warned me to slow down. "Don't overdo it, or you'll get a sore arm, Jack," he cautioned me.

But I couldn't slow down. Every time I heard somebody mumble, "Beautiful throw," I tried to throw the next one harder. When someone said, "Look at that stop," my rabbit ears picked up the comment and I strained myself to reach even farther to pick the ball out of the dirt.

My first realization of what I had done came when, after a hard peg, a burning sensation throbbed in my right arm. I kept throwing and leaping that day, however, because I didn't want Sukie to know that I was paying so quickly for my failure to heed his advice.

When I got home that night my arm felt as if it was being pulled out of the socket. I couldn't lift it to comb my hair. Rae tried desperately to help by putting on cold compresses. Still, I tossed and turned all night. Next morning Hopper hit a ball to me, but I couldn't throw it halfway to first. I went to the doctor, who put hot compresses on my arm, but still I couldn't throw. On top of that, I couldn't hit. The harder I tried the more I popped up or pounded the ball into the dirt, where the third baseman or shortstop gobbled it up easily and pegged me out at first. The more I tried the more tense I became. Rae almost became a nervous wreck trying to work the soreness out of my arm. She and I realized later that there is virtually nothing you can do about a sore arm except to let time work it out.

It was even more disturbing to find that Rae and I were not the only ones worried. Mr. Rickey was frantic to have me in the game, showing off my wares.

"Listen," he said, "you've *got* to get in there, sore arm or not. For anybody else it would be all right, but remember that you're here under extraordinary circumstances. You can't afford to miss a single day of practice or some of the other players will start rumors that you're goldbricking, that you're dogging off with the pretense that you have a sore arm."

He wanted Hopper to try me at second, where the throw to first would be much shorter. I tried that and found to my utter horror that I couldn't even throw from second to first.

Mr. Rickey dropped his head as if in despair. He called me over to the coaching box and told me that he had to keep me in the game even if he had to make a first baseman out of me. So he got me a first baseman's mitt and spent more than an hour showing me how to play the bag, and just what to do under certain conditions. I had no desire whatsoever to play first base, but I had to go along. In practice I felt awkward. I couldn't find the bag with my foot; I goofed easy throws. I was so horrible that one white newspaperman said:

"It's do-gooders like Rickey that hurt the Negro because they try to force inferior Negroes on whites and then everybody loses. Take this guy Robinson. If he was white they'd have booted him out of this camp long ago."

■Luckily, the soreness worked out of Jackie's arm as spring training progressed. Soon the team was traveling north. They were headed for Jersey City, New Jersey, where Montreal would open the regular season. When Jackie entered this game, it would be official—the color line in professional baseball would be broken. The question was no longer whether he would come to bat. Now the fans wanted to know if he could play. Seldom has a young athlete entered his first game under such pressure.

There was a lot of fanfare at Roosevelt Stadium. Mayor Frank Hague was there, with a lot of school children he had "liberated" by declaring a holiday. I remember the parades, the brass band's playing "The Star-Spangled Banner" and the marvelous beauty of this "day of destiny" for me. Nothing else mattered now—not even the people who, I now knew, had ordered me out of Sanford, not even the insults and humiliations, the days and nights of strain. None of this would show up in the records of the years to come—only the hits, runs and errors of this day. As they played "The Star-Spangled Banner" and Old Glory rolled slowly toward that azure blue sky, I stood on the base line with a lump in my throat and my heart beating rapidly, my stomach feeling as if it were full of feverish fireflies with claws on their feet. I was remembering what Mr. Rickey had said to me in spring training: "Jackie, we scouted you for a long time. So I know what you can do, and I want you to do it. I want you to run those bases like lightning. I want you to worry the daylights out of those pitchers. Don't be afraid to take a chance, to try to steal that extra base. Sure, sometimes you'll get caught but just remember this: I prefer the daring player to one who is afraid to take a chance. Just remember the best base runners get caught, even Ty Cobb. Just go out there and run like the devil."

Yes, I thought, how I'll run like the devil—if I can ever get on base!

The umpire shouted, "Play ball!" and the Jersey City team dashed onto the field to a deafening roar by fans who packed every seat in this stadium.

Breard stepped to the plate and I crouched on one knee in the batters' circle, awaiting my turn. I watched the pitcher closely, as Mr. Rickey had told me to do, so as to be able to get the jump on him when I decided to steal—if I got on. Breard slapped a grounder to shortstop and was thrown out. As I strode to the plate there was an ear-splitting roar. I felt weak in the knees. My palms felt too moist to grip the bat. I was afraid to look toward the stands for fear I would see only Negroes applauding—that the white fans would be sitting stony-faced, or yelling epithets.

The pitcher threw five times, I think, before I got the rubber out of my knees. Luckily the count was three balls and two strikes. When he threw again I swung with all my might and dribbled an easy grounder to the shortstop, who threw me out by at least four steps. Another loud roar came from the stands, and this time I could see that the great portion of the cheers were from Negro fans—apparently Negroes who had never before given two hoots about a baseball game, but who had come out in order to say that they were present on the historic day when the racial barriers were broken in organized baseball. Thus they hardly knew the difference between a safe hit and an easy ground-out to the shortstop.

I went back to the bench, unhappy, of course, that I had not gotten on base, yet a little relieved to get the ice broken, to be able to run down that base line in front of all those people and have nothing awful happen. After the third out of the inning, I trotted out to my position.

I prayed that before the day was over I might do something to justify the applause of those fans and the support given me by those sports writers who believed that baseball belonged to all the American people. While I stood daydreaming, thinking of what was happening to me and the nation that day, I heard the slap of the bat against the ball and "awakened" just in time to see the ball screeching along the grass between the first baseman and me. I dashed toward the ball as quickly as my reflexes would permit, but could do no better than wave. Duke Bouknight had just drilled a single into right field. I wondered how long I had daydreamed, whether I could have gotten that ball had I been more alert. I quickly rationalized that it was too well hit and too perfectly placed for me to get it.

We held Jersey City scoreless in the second inning. In our half of the third I found myself in the first clutch situation of my baseball career. There were two men on base as a result of a walk and a single and I knew what the people in the stands were wondering: "Can he hit when there are ducks on the pond?" "Can he deliver when the opposing pitcher is bearing down?"

I stepped to the plate determined to move those men. Word was already around that I was a good bunter, and Manager Hopper decided to try to outguess pitcher Warren Sandell. He figured that the Giants would be looking for me to sacrifice the two runners to second and third. Hopper guessed right, because Sandell's first pitch was a fast one, letter-high down the middle. I swung with all my might and knew when the bat met the ball that I really had connected. As I dashed toward first, the roar of the crowd told me that this one was going all the way. It sailed more than 340 feet over the left-field fence. I had hit my first homer and driven in my first three runs in organized baseball. I was so excited, so exhilarated, as I circled those bases that it seemed all the oxygen had left my brain and for a moment those stands were just a blur in front of me. As I crossed home plate two teammates were waiting to shake hands.

"Atta boy, Jackie. Atta boy," said one. "That's the old ball game right there."

I got a warm reception from the Royals as I returned to the bench. I peeked into the stands for a look at Rae, who was beaming broadly. I felt even better.

Jackie Robinson crosses home plate after his home run in the 1946 season opener at Jersey City.

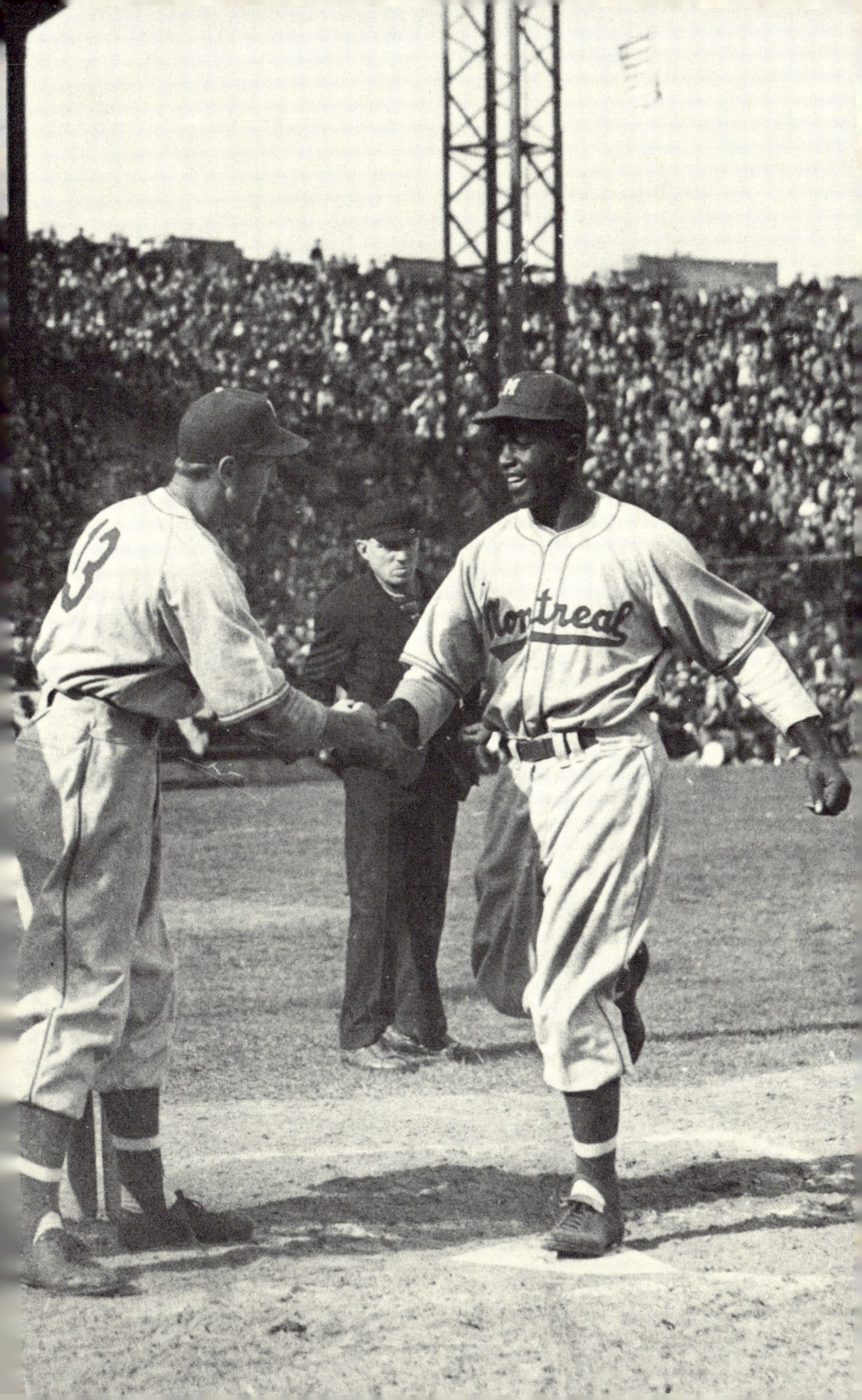
Montreal

196 ■ THE GUTS NOT TO FIGHT BACK

When I came up in the fifth inning I decided to cross up the Jersey City team. Instead of trying to slam the ball over the fence, I dropped a bunt down the third base line that caught the third baseman flatfooted. By the time he reached the slowly dribbling ball I had crossed first base. I remembered Mr. Rickey's advice to run those bases like crazy, so as the pitcher took his stretch I dashed daringly off first, then plunged back on my belly as the catcher faked a throw to first. When the pitcher began his stretch for the second pitch I dashed off recklessly again, but I kept going this time and stole second easily.

I dashed off second now, still trying to worry Larry Higgins, the New Jersey pitcher. He broke off an inside curve which Tom Tatum slapped hard on the ground to the third baseman. A standard rule in baseball is that a man on second does not try to advance when the ball is hit to third base or shortstop. I acted as if I were going back to second, but when third baseman Norm Jaeger threw to first I dashed toward third. The first baseman fired right back to Jaeger, but I slid into third, beating the throw by an eyelash. I had now stolen one base officially, and had "taken" third, although it never would appear in the record as a stolen base. I figured now was the time to be daring. I would try to steal home!

Phil Otis came in to pitch for Jersey City. After his warm-up throws, I began to dance down the base line. He looked toward home plate, then threw hard to third, but I slid back in safely. I danced down the line and he threw to third again, but I slid back safely. I knew now that Otis was worried. He watched me closely and then fired to the plate as I ran halfway down the base line, dashing back to third before the catcher could throw me out. On the next pitch I again dashed down the base line. Otis was so frustrated that he stopped his delivery toward home plate—a balk. The umpire waved me on to the plate and a score.

Now the crowd went wild. Not just the Negroes, but thousands of whites, including many Jersey City fans, screamed, laughed and stamped their feet, and I knew that this was no tribute to a Negro; this was people proving Mr. Rickey right: they liked daring baseball.

■Jackie's performance was truly spectacular. Montreal won 14-1, and Robinson had four hits, including the home run, in five times at bat. He had stolen two bases and scored four runs. His first game in white baseball was a stunning success.

Jackie soon became a hero to the Montreal fans, but he was taunted by fans and ballplayers in Baltimore and other cities in the league. Near the end of the season he came close to having a nervous breakdown from the continuing stress of being a black man in a white sport.

The next year, 1947, Jackie played for the Brooklyn Dodgers, breaking the color line in the major leagues. One team threatened to go on strike rather than play against Robinson. But the strike failed when the National League's president threatened to throw any uncooperative players out of baseball. As the season wore on, Jackie proved that he could keep his control and play exciting, aggressive baseball. He was named Rookie of the Year and the Dodgers won the pennant.

By 1949 there were many other black players in the major leagues and the pressure on Jackie let up. Rickey gave him permission to talk back and fight back, and Robinson responded by having the best year of his career. The Dodgers won the pennant again and Jackie was named the league's Most Valuable Player. He had proved in four short seasons that black players really did belong in organized baseball.

Today, when professional sports are filled with great black athletes, it is difficult to imagine what courage it took to be the first. Yet the performance of this one young athlete under immense pressure—his ability to ignore his tormentors and get revenge by playing well—made it easier for black men in and out of sport to claim their equality.

ABOUT THE AUTHOR

For more than five years, Lawrence T. Lorimer has been an editor of sports books for young readers, occasionally editing adult sports books and other juvenile nonfiction titles as well. *Breaking In* represents his first effort as an author. Mr. Lorimer was born in Denver, Colorado, and went to high school in Pasadena, California. After graduating from Augustana College in Rock Island, Illinois, he moved to New York City. There he began his career in publishing, taking time out to earn a master's degree in English literature at Columbia University. At present, he and his wife Janice stay fit by keeping up with their two very energetic children, Paul and Judith.